RAF
TYPHOON

COVER CUTAWAY: **RAF Typhoon** (Mike Badrocke)

ENDPAPERS
FRONT: **Typhoon T1, ZJ802, of 29 Squadron, lands at Coningsby.** (Chris Wood)
REAR: **Typhoon F2, ZJ931, of 11 Squadron.** (Lloyd Horgan)

First published in June 2013
Reprinted July 2018

A catalogue record for this book is available from the British Library

ISBN 978 085733 075 8

Library of Congress control no. 2013932252

Published by Haynes Publishing,
Sparkford, Yeovil,
Somerset BA22 7JJ, UK.
Tel: 01963 440635
Int. tel: +44 1963 440635
Website: www.haynes.com

Haynes North America Inc.
859 Lawrence Drive, Newbury Park,
California 91320, USA.

Printed in Malaysia.

Acknowledgements

No book is ever the work of a single person. My name might be on the cover, but this book stands as testament to the industriousness and efforts of a whole team of people, each of whom is essential to the project's existence.

First and foremost, I'd like to thank the members of the RAF who made this work possible: Squadron Leader Stuart Balfour MBE, whose inspiration and support saw this project given wings, and Squadron Leader John McFall at the MoD who picked up the baton and ran with it; also, Wing Commander Mark Quinn for going far and beyond the call of duty in tirelessly responding to my every query, often at short notice; and Wing Commander Roger Elliott at Typhoon Force HQ. For everything that all of you have done, thank you.

Special thanks to Carol; for your patience, believing in me, putting up with the inconvenience, and for the endless support. I couldn't have done it without you.

Thanks too, to my friend Jonathan Falconer, and all at Haynes Publishing who saw the potential in this book from the very beginning. Jonathan, it's been fun as always and I can't thank you enough for your support, enthusiasm, and sheer hard work.

I'm indebted to the Ministry of Defence and its staff for supporting and believing in this project, and to several people at RAF Coningsby who were instrumental in my getting access to and talking to the people I needed to reach. To Wing Commander Paul Godfrey, Jim Robinson, Pete the photographer and countless others at the RAF's spiritual home to Typhoon, thank you. And to Nick Robinson; thanks for everything – it's always a pleasure working with you.

Thanks also to Kathryn Holm at Eurofighter for her prompt, cheery responses and willingness to help.

Huge thanks to my friends and family who have supported me throughout.

The final word must go to all those serving officers, NCOs and technicians who I spent time talking to and who contributed their experiences to create this book. I couldn't have done it without you. Thank you all.

RAF TYPHOON

1994 Onwards (all models)

Haynes

ⓘ ROYAL
AIR FORCE
OFFICIAL LICENSED PRODUCT

Owner's Manual

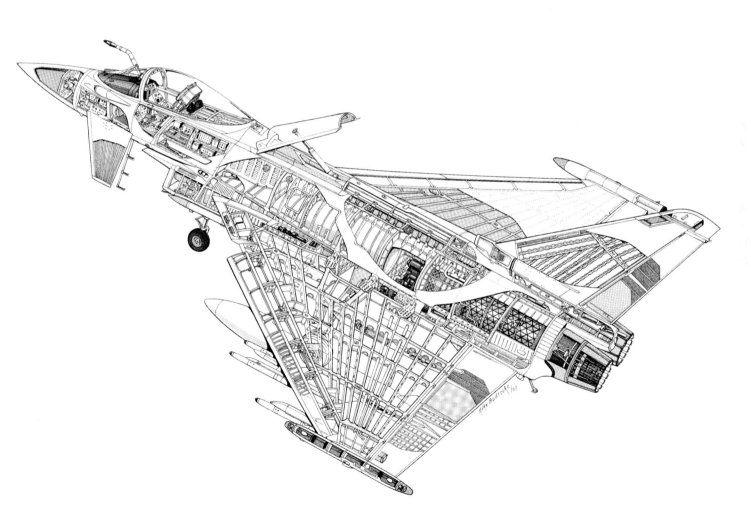

An insight into owning, flying and maintaining the world's most advanced multi-role fast-jet

Antony Loveless

Contents

OPPOSITE **No 1435 Flight Typhoon over the South Atlantic around the Falkland Islands.** *(RAF)*

Author's note

There has never been a Haynes Manual like this one because Haynes has never previously commissioned one on a vehicle as cutting-edge as the Typhoon. This state-of-the-art multi-role combat aircraft is as advanced as it gets.

If you're expecting a traditional Haynes Manual with an engineering bias and an in-depth analysis 'under the hood', you'll be both disappointed and inspired. Disappointed, because this aircraft doesn't really do 'mechanical' in the conventional sense. Inspired, because the Typhoon redraws the boundaries.

The RAF engineers who look after this aircraft refer to it as 'plug and play'. They're not so much mechanics as technicians and software engineers. Because in 90% of cases where a system or display fails, they do exactly what you or I would do whenever a computer program misbehaves: 'Ctrl-Alt-Delete'.

Rebooting whichever system is at fault almost always solves the problem. And on the rare occasions that a problem lies deeper, it's simply a matter of connecting the aircraft to a diagnostic unit (much like an auto technician does when your car's engine management warning light has illuminated). That informs the technician which black box needs to be replaced with another and then it's simply a matter of swapping them. Plug and play.

The Typhoon is, as you will discover, a truly remarkable aircraft, marrying the most cutting-edge production techniques and materials with state-of-the-art technology. The result is the most advanced, manoeuvrable and efficient multi-role combat aircraft currently in service anywhere. Its manoeuvrability is born of its relaxed stability design. In aviation, relaxed stability is the tendency of an aircraft to change its attitude and angle of bank of its own accord. What it means is that the Typhoon is designed to be inherently unstable; it takes 70 on-board computers just to keep it flying.

The upside is that it makes the aircraft highly agile at both supersonic and low speeds. A quadruplex digital fly-by-wire control system provides the pilot with an artificial stability that manual operation alone could never provide.

Everything about the Typhoon is cutting-edge. Its airframe is built using the latest low-weight, high-strength composite materials. Carbon Fibre Composite (CFC) makes up 70% of the airframe structure; a further 15% is metal (Titanium and Aluminium alloys) and the remainder is constructed using 12% Glass Reinforced Plastic (GRP) and 3% acrylics.

The Typhoon's delta-wing configuration and unusual foreplane stability give the aircraft amazing agility, high lift and STOL (Short Take-Off and Landing) performance while still maintaining a low drag coefficient. The Typhoon is equipped with a wide array of sensors including the ECR90 radar and an advanced integrated Defensive Aids System (DAS) for self-defence. The pilot can carry out many aircraft functions using the 'Hand-On Throttle And Stick' (HOTAS) and voice-activated commands whilst simultaneously manoeuvring the aircraft.

The Typhoon can supercruise faster than

BELOW A dual-seat 29 (R) Squadron Typhoon T1 climbs to altitude on a combat take-off. Combat take-offs see the aircraft airborne over shorter distances due to the use of max reheat (clearly visible here).
(Clare Scott)

the speed of sound without the need for reheat due to the phenomenal performance of the EJ200 engines. With a thrust-to-weight ratio in excess of 1.2:1, a fully-armed and laden Typhoon can accelerate at low level from 200 knots (370km/h) to Mach 1.0 (the speed of sound, around 1225km/h) in just 30 seconds. The aircraft's 13 armament hard points and gun can be utilised to carry a vast array of ordnance from the NATO inventory including the latest air-to-air and air-to-surface weapons.

With 2011's Operation Ellamy, which saw RAF Typhoons deployed in anger for the first time as part of the UK's involvement in military action in Libya, the aircraft proved itself in an operational environment. It has already replaced the Tornado F3s on Quick Reaction Alert (QRA), the 24-hour-a-day, 365-days-a-year deterrent that sees armed Typhoons on standby to intercept threats to UK airspace. There is a permanent detachment of Typhoons in the Falklands, as the spearhead of Britain's defence of the Islands. And throughout the Olympic Games in London in summer 2012, there was a detachment of Typhoons at RAF Northolt ready to protect the skies over the capital.

With Typhoon the RAF has, for the first time in its history, a proven combat aircraft capable of being deployed across the full spectrum of air operations. From air policing and peace support all the way through to high-intensity conflict, the Typhoon can do it all. This exceptionally flexible and capable aircraft has significantly increased the RAF's war-fighting capability.

What this book will do is give you an in-depth insight into just what makes the Typhoon such a potent weapons platform; it will open the door to how it works, what it's like to fly and operate, and what it takes to keep it flying.

Because it is such a recent addition to the RAF's fleet, there are elements about the Typhoon that, for reasons of operational or national security, can't be disclosed. However, these are minor and won't detract from this book giving you a powerful insight into what this incredible aircraft is really like.

Come and enjoy the journey.

ABOVE This 3 (F) Squadron Typhoon displays the squadron's 100th anniversary commemorative paint scheme, applied to the aircraft to mark the formation of the squadron at Larkhill on 13 May 1912. *(Lloyd Horgan)*

Chapter One

The Typhoon story

———(●)————————————

The supersonic Eurofighter Typhoon embodies a revolution in aerospace technology. Developed and built by Europe's largest military collaborative programme, it is the world's most advanced new generation multi-role/ swing-role combat aircraft. Since 2004, more than 350 Eurofighter Typhoons have been delivered to six nations: Germany, the United Kingdom, Italy, Spain, Austria and Saudi Arabia. In 2012 Oman became the seventh customer to order the aircraft.

OPPOSITE **Typhoon from 3 (F) Squadron on Exercise 'Taurus Mountain', a Quick Reaction Alert (QRA) training sortie over UK airspace.** *(RAF)*

OPPOSITE The Typhoon has eclipsed the Tornado in the air defence role. A Typhoon F2 (top) from 11 Squadron, Coningsby, in close formation with a Tornado F3 aircraft formerly from the same squadron. As the multi-role lead squadron, 11 Squadron spearheaded the development of the Typhoon's air-to-surface capability, which was ready for deployed operations by the summer of 2008. *(RAF)*

The Eurofighter Typhoon FGR4 (Fighter/Ground-attack/Reconnaissance) is the world's most advanced swing-role combat aircraft and, on 1 July 2008, it became the first and only current RAF fast jet to be declared multi-role capable. As with the RAF's other fast jets, the Typhoon can deliver its weapons quickly and accurately; however, it's unique in being able to utilise its own inherent air-to-air capability to fight its way to the target and back again without having to rely on additional dedicated fighters for protection. It's also capable of delivering its weapons as a close air support platform in aid of troops on the ground.

Genesis

The Typhoon doesn't just nudge aside the aging Tornado F3 – the fighter jet it replaces – it completely obliterates it. Developed in the last few years of the 1960s, the Tornado was the true embodiment of Cold War technology, but viewed through the lens of hindsight, it is mechanical, ungainly and technologically moribund. Conceived as a long-range interceptor to replace the Lightning F6 and Phantom FGR2, it was introduced in 1986 to counter the threat posed by the large Soviet long-range bomber fleet, in particular the supersonic Tupolev Tu-22M.

Compared with the Tornado, Typhoon isn't just an evolution but a revolution. Its genesis represents everything that modern technology has to offer but perhaps its strongest attribute is that it has been designed to be 'future proof'. As new technologies come online, Typhoon has been designed so that they can be fully integrated into its existing infrastructure, rather than 'bolted on' and retrofitted as has happened with previous generations of aircraft.

Even as initial development work began in 1971 on what would become the Tornado, a requirement for a new UK fighter jet was identified. From the very earliest days of its conception, the project that was destined to become the Eurofighter Typhoon was designed as a multi-role/swing-role platform. Its earliest iteration resulted in a conventional 'tailed' design that was presented in the late 1970s – around the time that the Tornado was making its maiden flight.

ABOVE AND RIGHT Typhoons destined for the Royal Air Force are assembled at BAE Systems' British Aerospace's final assembly facility at Warton in Lancashire. Warton was used as the base for all British development aircraft in the Eurofighter programme. *(BAE Systems and Geoff Lee/Eurofighter)*

OPPOSITE Luftwaffe Typhoons at the EADS final assembly facility at Manching. Final assembly of Eurofighter, system tests, flight-testing and in-service support for aircraft flown by the German Air Force is all done at EADS' Manching HQ in Bavaria. *(Geoff Lee/ Eurofighter)*

Although the design met the MoD's requirements, it was too similar to the McDonnell Douglas F/A-18 Hornet, which by then was well advanced in its development. It was felt that the design had little potential for future growth as, by the time it entered production, the vital export market would have been sewn up by the well-established Hornet.

A simultaneous West German requirement for a new fighter had led by 1979 to the development of a concept known as the TKF-90 which featured a cranked delta-wing design with forward canard controls and artificial stability. Although designers at British Aerospace rejected some of its advanced features, they agreed with the overall configuration.

Later that year, Messerschmitt-Bölkow-Blohm (MBB) and British Aerospace (BAE) presented a formal proposal to their respective governments for the ECF – the European Collaborative Fighter or European Combat Fighter – and later that year Dassault joined the ECF team for a tri-national study, which became known as the European Combat Aircraft. It was at this stage of development that the Eurofighter name was first attached to the aircraft.

In Turin on 2 August 1985, the UK, West Germany and Italy agreed to go ahead with the Eurofighter and confirmed that France, along with Spain, had chosen not to proceed. Spain wavered however and despite pressure from the French, rejoined the Eurofighter project just a month later. France officially withdrew to pursue development of its ACX project, a design which eventually came into service in 2000 as the Dassault Rafale.

The agreement which formed the basis of the Eurofighter's development programme defined the requirement for an extremely agile fighter that would dominate the skies to the mid-21st century – a single-seat, twin-engine fighter with optimal performance in Beyond Visual Range (BVR) and close combat, with significant ground attack capabilities. The

RIGHT Final assembly of the 180 Eurofighters destined for the German Air Force began in December 2000. The first production Eurofighter for Germany took off on its maiden flight in February 2003. *(Geoff Lee/Eurofighter)*

inherent flexibility of the final design means that an extended role to encompass air-to-surface capability can also be achieved without affecting the aircraft's air superiority.

In 1986, a multinational company called Eurofighter Jagdflugzeug GmbH was established in Munich to co-ordinate the design, development and production of the aircraft which became known as Eurofighter EFA. The company is made up of the major aerospace companies of the four Eurofighter partner nations and is responsible for delivering the Eurofighter weapon system to the NATO Eurofighter and Tornado Management Agency (NETMA). NETMA represents the Eurofighter partner nations' governments and was established to oversee the procurement of the Eurofighter Typhoon and its related weapon systems into their respective air forces.

Alongside Eurofighter GmbH are two partner consortiums set up in the same way, for the same purpose: EuroJet Turbo GmbH is an alliance between Rolls-Royce (UK), Avio (Italy), ITP (Spain) and MTU Aero Engines (Germany) that was established to develop the EJ200 engine for the new fighter aircraft. EuroRadar is a consortium brought together to design, develop and produce the advanced Captor radar, comprised of SELEX Galileo (UK and Italy), EADS Defence Electronics (Germany) and INDRA (Spain).

Any multi-role aircraft is always going to be a compromise between its ground-attack and air-to-air roles, and having four nations with slightly differing requirements was always likely to

RIGHT BAE Systems' Test Pilot, Mark Bowman, is based at Warton, Lancashire. *(BAE Systems)*

BELOW BAE Systems' DA4 landing with brake chute at Warton. The aircraft is loaded with ASRAAM and AMRAAM missiles. *(Geoff Lee/Eurofighter)*

OPPOSITE TOP
**Arrival and off-loading
of Typhoon BS037,
first RAF tranche II,
in 302H Typhoon final
assembly.**
(BAE Systems)

OPPOSITE BOTTOM
**Austrian Air Force
Eurofighters based at
Zeltweg. They have
IRIS-T missiles.** *(Geoff
Lee/Eurofighter)*

complicate things still further, so it was agreed early on that air superiority requirements would drive the aerodynamic design of the airframe. The design concept evolved after the collapse of the Soviet Union so the requirement, role and capabilities had to be reoriented to take into account the changing requirements of the post-Cold War defence environment.

The construction of the first Eurofighter prototypes began in 1989 and the prototype's first maiden flight took place in Bavaria in 1994. It was agreed that each of the four parent nations would host the production line and final assembly for the components of the aircraft it was responsible for: For the UK, the Warton home of BAE Systems; Manching for EADS Germany; Turin for Alenia Aeronautica in Italy; and Getafe for EADS CASA in Spain.

A programme milestone was reached in December 1997 when the Memoranda of Understanding (MoU) covering production and support was signed by the four defence ministers in Bonn. NETMA and Eurofighter GmbH subsequently signed the initial production and support contracts for the purchase of 620 aircraft on 30 January 1998. The procurement totals saw the UK committed to purchasing 232 aircraft, Germany 180, Italy

121, and Spain 87. Production was allotted according to procurement: British Aerospace (37.42%), DASA (29.03%), Aeritalia (19.52%), and CASA (14.03%).

On 2 September 1998, a naming ceremony was held at Farnborough. This saw the Typhoon name formally adopted, although it was reportedly resisted by Germany – their objection was apparently due to sensitivity over the Hawker Typhoon, the fighter-bomber used by the RAF against Germany during World War Two. The name Spitfire II was also considered and rejected for the same reason early in the development programme.

Tranches

To take in to account the growth potential of the aircraft and the possibility to insert new capabilities in the future, the decision was taken to divide production of the aircraft into three Tranches: the first one for 148 aircraft, the second and the third for 236 each. Tranche 1 encompassed production between 2003 and 2007, Tranche 2 between 2007 and 2012, with Tranche 3 aircraft to be produced between 2013 and 2018.

The contract for the engines, foreseen to

total 1,382 EJ200s, was also split accordingly to match the three aircraft production tranches.

The Tranche 1 contract for the Eurofighter Typhoon aircraft was signed on 18 September 1998. This fixed-price contract covered the production of the first Tranche of 148 aircraft for a value of about €7 billion.

Work on the sub-assemblies for the first series production Eurofighter aircraft had commenced in late 1998 and deliveries started in summer 2003 when over 100 aircraft were at various stages of production at the four partner companies' assembly lines. The first Eurofighter Typhoon aircraft were accepted by the four air forces between 2003 and the beginning of 2004. The first one went to the Luftwaffe; then to the RAF, which kept its first aircraft in Warton for flying training; third to receive its aircraft was the Spanish *Ejercito de l'Aire*; and finally the Italian *Aeronautica Militare* received its first aircraft. The aircraft entered into service with all four nations in Spring 2004.

In July 2003, Eurofighter GmbH signed its first export contract, when Austria reached an agreement for the delivery of 18 aircraft to start in 2007. This contract was revised in 2007, after a budget review, and the delivery of 15 aircraft of Tranche 1 standard was finally agreed.

On 14 December 2004 Eurofighter and NETMA signed the Tranche 2 production contract – worth €13 billion – for 236 aircraft, thus confirming Eurofighter's position of having the largest order book of any next-generation fighter aircraft.

In 2007 came a second export success for the Eurofighter Typhoon with an important contract signed by the UK government with Saudi Arabia for the delivery of 72 Tranche 2 production standard aircraft to the Kingdom of Saudi Arabia Air Force. It was agreed that the first 24 aircraft, manufactured by BAE Systems, would be drawn from the batch assigned to the RAF and then replaced by new production aircraft. The first aircraft for KSA was delivered in June 2009.

The year 2009 marked another important step in the programme's history as on 31 July the four nations of the Eurofighter consortium signed the contract for the first part of the Tranche 3 production aircraft (112 units) for a value, engines included, of €9 billion.

OPPOSITE Saudi Arabia announced it had signed a £4.4bn deal with BAE Systems for 72 Eurofighter Typhoons on 17 September 2007. A first tranche of 24 were delivered to the Saudi Royal Air Force on 11 August 2011. *(Katsuhiko Tokunaga/ Eurofighter)*

Chapter Two

Anatomy of the Typhoon

With an airframe constructed mainly from Carbon Fibre Composites, lightweight alloys, titanium and Glass Reinforced Plastics, low observability technology is a feature of the Typhoon's delta-wing design. Married to state-of-the art avionics, a low wing loading and a high thrust-to-weight ratio, the result is a combat aircraft with a mind-blowing capability, acceleration and agility.

OPPOSITE A rear view of one of the Typhoon's EuroJet EJ200 engines. Its reheat (afterburner) system provides thrust augmentation. Visible here is its variable area final nozzle, which is a convergent-divergent design. *(Author)*

The Eurofighter Typhoon is unique among modern combat aircraft in having four separate assembly lines. Each partner company assembles its own national aircraft, but builds the same parts for all 683 aircraft (including exports).

The airframe is designed to last 6,000 hours, which equates to 30 years of service. In September 1998 static testing of the airframe was completed with a simulated 18,000 hours on the clock, or three times the design's expected life.

General description

The Eurofighter Typhoon FGR4 is a single/dual-seat multi-role fast jet. The aircraft comprises a foreplane/delta-wing configuration that is aerodynamically unstable at subsonic speeds. The delta canard design of the aircraft is driven by a need for:

- Instantaneous and sustained turn rate performance at both sub and supersonic speeds
- Agility
- Lift and STOL (Short Take-Off and Landing)
- Exceptional acceleration
- Reduced drag

All of this, combined with a low wing loading, high thrust-to-weight ratio, excellent all-round vision and carefree handling means that Typhoon is a truly exceptional aircraft.

Although not classed as a stealth fighter, the Typhoon's design team took measures to ensure that its radar cross section was as low as practicable; you could say that low observability technology is incorporated in the basic design. The combination of low visual detection, low radar reflection, use of passive systems, defensive aids, secure communications and the capability of supercruise supported by a cockpit that gives the pilot a clear tactical picture and continuous and instant control over the level of emissions from the aircraft, ensure that the Eurofighter Typhoon has high survivability and the ability to operate independently from ground and airborne control agencies in dense electronic warfare environments.

Materials

The Typhoon benefits from significant advances in recent years in the fields of metallurgy, polymer science and composites. It's not just under the skin that the aircraft is cutting edge – over 80% of the Typhoon's airframe is comprised of modern materials, which leads to a far smoother surface finish compared with that offered by metal structures. This is a significant contributing factor to the Typhoon's low radar cross-section, with the additional benefit of a higher strength-to-weight ratio compared with the aircraft's predecessors.

Typhoon's airframe is constructed mainly from Carbon Fibre Composites (CFCs), lightweight alloys, titanium and Glass Reinforced Plastics (GRP).

The airframe surface area is made of 70% Carbon Fibre Composites (CFCs), 15% lightweight alloys and titanium, 12% Glass Reinforced Plastics (GRP) and 3% other materials. In other words, metals make up only 15% of the materials used in building each Eurofighter Typhoon. The use of these strong but lightweight materials means that the airframe and engine are up to 20% smaller and 30% lighter than those of the Typhoon's predecessors. This contributes to the aircraft's stealth capabilities through its reduced radar signature.

Who makes what?

Premium AEROTEC in Germany manufactures the main centre fuselage; EADS CASA in Spain makes the right wing and leading edge slats; Alenia Aeronautica of Italy provides the left wing, outboard flaperons and rear fuselage sections; and BAE Systems is responsible for provision of the front fuselage (including foreplanes), the canopy, dorsal spine, tail fin, inboard flaperons and rear fuselage section.

ABOVE An XI Squadron Typhoon FGR4. The Typhoon's airframe is constructed mainly from modern materials such as Carbon Fibre Composites (CFCs), lightweight alloys, titanium and Glass Reinforced Plastic (GRP). *(RAF)*

EUROFIGHTER TYPHOON CUTAWAY.

(Mike Badrocke)

1 Glass fibre reinforced plastic (GFRP) radome, hinged to starboard for access
2 ECR-90 multi-mode pulse-doppler radar scanner
3 Scanner tracking mechanism
4 Retractable flight refuelling probe
5 Instrument panel shroud
6 Forward-looking infra-red seeker
7 Radar equipment bay
8 Air data sensor
9 Port canard foreplane
10 Foreplane diffusion-bonded titanium structure
11 Foreplane hinge mounting
12 Hydraulic actuator
13 Rudder pedals
14 Instrument panel with full colour multi-function head-down displays (HDD)

15 Head-up display (HUD)
16 Rear view mirrors
17 Upward-hinging cockpit canopy
18 Pilot's Martin-Baker Mk 16a 'zero-zero' ejection seat
19 Control column handgrip, full-authority digital active-control technology (ACT) fly-by-wire control system
20 Engine throttle levers, HOTAS controls
21 Side console panel
22 Boarding steps, extended
23 Boundary layer splitter

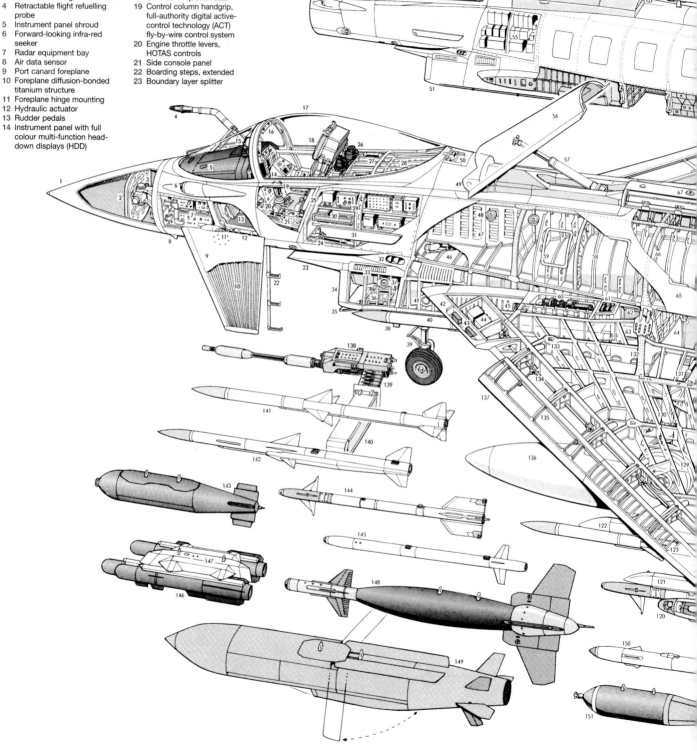

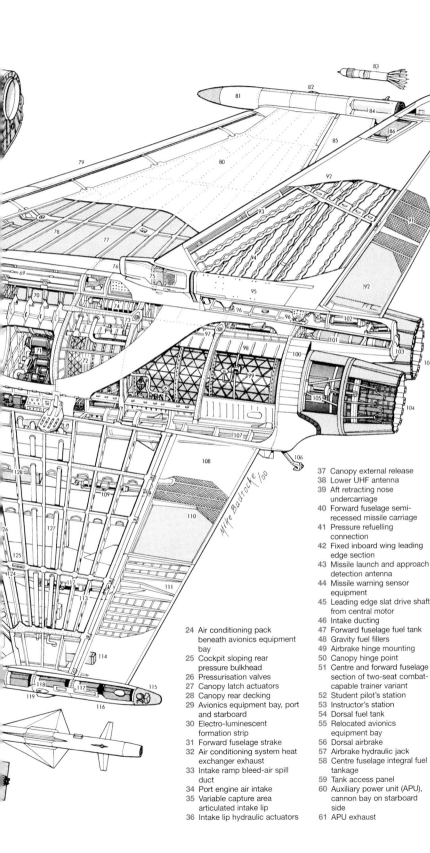

100 Tailpipe sealing plates
101 Brake parachute housing
102 Rudder hydraulic actuator
103 Parachute hinged door
104 Variable area afterburner nozzle
105 Nozzle actuator
106 Runway emergency arrestor hook
107 Aft fuselage semi-recessed missile carriage
108 Port elevon all-CFC structure
109 Inboard elevon hydraulic actuator
110 Elevon honeycomb core structure
111 Outboard elevon all-titanium structure
112 Outboard elevon hydraulic actuator
113 Actuator ventral fairings
114 Outboard pylon countermeasures dispenser
115 Aft ECM/ESM antennae
116 Wing tip electronic-countermeasures/electronic surveillance (ECM/ESM) pod
117 Formation lighting strip
118 Port navigation light
119 Equipment cooling ram-air intake
120 Forward ECM/ESM antennae
121 Outboard missile pylon
122 Port wing leading-edge two-segment slat
123 Intermediate stores pylon
124 Pylon mounting hardpoints
125 Port wing integral fuel tankage
126 Wing panel multi-panel structure
127 Cable conduits
128 Elevon hinge fairing-mounted countermeasures dispensers
129 Port main wheel
130 Mainwheel shock-absorber leg strut
131 Hydraulic retraction jack
132 Undercarriage leg mounting stub spars
133 Wing root pylon-mounting hardpoint
134 Leading edge slat operating screw jacks and torque shaft
135 Slat guide rails
136 330 Imp gal (1,500-litre) external fuel tank
137 Wing leading edge slat extended position
138 Mauser BK27, 27mm cannon
139 Ammunition feed chute
140 Ammunition magazine, 150 rounds
141 AIM-120 AMRAAM, advanced medium-range air-to-air missile
142 Meteor FMRAAM, future advanced medium-range air-to-air missile
143 BL-755 cluster bomb
144 AIM-9L Sidewinder, short-range air-to-air missile
145 IRIS-T, close-range air-to-air missile
146 Brimstone air-to-surface anti-armour missiles
147 Three-round missile carrier/launcher
148 GBU-24/B Paveway III, 2,000lb laser-guided bomb
149 MBDA Storm Shadow, stand-off precision-guided attack weapon
150 MBDA ALARM, air-launched anti-radiation missile
151 454kg (1,000lb) HE bomb, No 117 retarded version

62 Cannon ammunition magazine
63 Titanium wing panel attachment fittings
64 Main undercarriage wheel bay
65 Carbon fibre composite (CFC) centre fuselage skin panelling
66 Machined wing attachment fuselage main frames
67 Anti-collision strobe light
68 TACAN antenna
69 Dorsal spine fairing air and cable ducting
70 Centre section integral fuel tankage
71 Secondary power system equipment bay, engine-driven engine-mounted accessory equipment gearboxes
72 EuroJet EJ200 afterburning low-bypass turbofan engine
73 Forward engine mounting
74 Hydraulic reservoir, dual system, port and starboard
75 Engine bleed-air primary heat exchanger
76 Heat exchanger ram-air intake
77 Starboard wing panel integral fuel tankage
78 Wing tank fire-suppressant reticulated foam filling
79 Starboard leading edge slat segment
80 Wing CFC skin panel
81 Starboard wingtip EW pod
82 Starboard navigation light
83 Towed radar decoy (TRD)
84 Decoy housing (2) in rear of EW pod
85 Starboard outboard elevon
86 HF antenna
87 Upper UHF/IFF antenna
88 Rear position light
89 Fuel jettison
90 Rudder
91 Rudder honeycomb core structure
92 Fin and rudder CFC skin panels
93 Electro-luminescent formation lighting strip
94 Fin CFC 'sine-wane' spar structure
95 Heat exchanger titanium exhaust shield
96 Fin attachment joints
97 Rear engine mounting
98 Engine bay thermal lining
99 Afterburner ducting

37 Canopy external release
38 Lower UHF antenna
39 Aft retracting nose undercarriage
40 Forward fuselage semi-recessed missile carriage
41 Pressure refuelling connection
42 Fixed inboard wing leading edge section
43 Missile launch and approach detection antenna
44 Missile warning sensor equipment
45 Leading edge slat drive shaft from central motor
46 Intake ducting
47 Forward fuselage fuel tank
48 Gravity fuel fillers
49 Airbrake hinge mounting
50 Canopy hinge point
51 Centre and forward fuselage section of two-seat combat-capable trainer variant
52 Student pilot's station
53 Instructor's station
54 Dorsal fuel tank
55 Relocated avionics equipment bay
56 Dorsal airbrake
57 Airbrake hydraulic jack
58 Centre fuselage integral fuel tankage
59 Tank access panel
60 Auxiliary power unit (APU), cannon bay on starboard side
61 APU exhaust

24 Air conditioning pack beneath avionics equipment bay
25 Cockpit sloping rear pressure bulkhead
26 Pressurisation valves
27 Canopy latch actuators
28 Canopy rear decking
29 Avionics equipment bay, port and starboard
30 Electro-luminescent formation strip
31 Forward fuselage strake
32 Air conditioning system heat exchanger exhaust
33 Intake ramp bleed-air spill duct
34 Port engine air intake
35 Variable capture area articulated intake lip
36 Intake lip hydraulic actuators

ABOVE AND ABOVE RIGHT The Typhoon's bird-proof acrylic bubble canopy (an FGR4 canopy is seen here) is one of the largest in its class; only the USAF's F-22 Raptor has a larger canopy. Its clear, unobstructed design gives the pilot almost 360° visibility (the view is from the cockpit of a T3). *(Author)*

RIGHT AND BELOW There are two canopy variants for the Typhoon: the single-piece twin-cockpit canopy measures 2.7m, and is one of the largest ever produced for a military aircraft. The single-cockpit variant is marginally shorter at 2.6m. *(RAF)*

Canopy

One factor that gives the Typhoon an advantage in air-to-air combat performance is its cockpit's exceptional field of view. The bird-proof acrylic bubble canopy is one of the largest and best in its class, giving the pilot 360° vision outside his cockpit with a 40° look-down angle over the side of the aircraft, and 15° over the nose (compared to the more common 12° or 13° of previous aircraft); the pilot's seat is elevated for this purpose. Only the USAF's F-22 Raptor has a larger canopy.

Bubble canopies give the pilot a much wider field of view than flush canopies, such as those seen on early fighter aircraft, which left a conspicuous blind spot behind that enemy pilots could exploit to sneak up unseen.

The 2.7m single-piece canopy for the two-seat version of the Typhoon is one of the largest produced for a military aircraft. The canopy for the single-seat aircraft is only marginally shorter at 2.6m. Its simplicity and the clarity it offers mask the complexity involved in its design and production due to the complex and sometimes competing functions it needs to provide. These encompass pressure, fatigue, resistance to bird strike and crew escape.

In event of the pilot having to eject from the aircraft, the canopy is jettisoned by two rocket motors.

Fuselage

The Typhoon's fuselage comprises several sections, which break down as follows:

Front fuselage

The front fuselage includes: the cockpit area and canopy/windscreen; foreplane actuators; a fully retractable flight refuelling probe; the radar infra-red sensor; and avionics and Environmental Control Systems (ECS) bays. A hydraulically operated air-brake is integrated behind the cockpit, moving into a near-vertical position to maximise drag when required.

Centre fuselage

The aluminium chin intake has an upper surface wedge, vertical splitter plate and external walls with flow bleed arrangements incorporated. A variable lower cowl lip optimises intake performance.

The main body includes fuel tanks, the secondary power system, part of the main undercarriage bay, the major wing pick-ups

BELOW A single-seat RAF Typhoon FGR4 ready for take-off. Clearly visible are the aircraft's foreplanes, its radar infra-red sensor, and its radar-housing nose cone assembly. *(RAF)*

and the internal gun. Mainframes are of aluminium lithium with extensive use of CFC for external skins.

Separating the engine bays is a vertical shear web manufactured from superplastically-formed and diffusion-bonded titanium. Two large engine bay doors are fitted and form the underside structure of the fuselage. Where temperature permits, CFC is used for external panels.

Rear fuselage

There are two major frames supporting the engines. The rear frame also incorporates fin and arrester hook attachments.

Refuelling probe

A fighter jet's Achilles' heel is its range. By design, fighter aircraft are light, fast and manoeuvrable – all traits that mean the aircraft's

fuel capacity must be limited. The Typhoon is restricted to sorties of between one and one-and-a-half hours without refuelling and its range falls further depending on the nature of the sortie.

The ability to stay on station enhances any aircraft's capabilities and to enable this, the Typhoon is equipped with a standard retractable NATO refuelling probe. The system is mounted within a small starboard compartment just below the canopy. This gives the pilot excellent visibility during refuelling operations. In an emergency fuel can be jettisoned through a tail-mounted ejector pipe.

To undertake missions of the duration seen in Libya – up to eight hours – the Typhoon needed three air-to-air refuellings. The Typhoon is equipped with data-sharing technology that enables command and control aircraft, such

as Sentry (AWACS), to monitor an individual aircraft's fuel and weapon payload, which enables aircraft to be matched to suitable targets as well as managing the complex task of aerial refuelling.

Air intakes

The Typhoon's air intakes are positioned below the aircraft in a design cue that owes much to the F-16. Their placement ensures an uninterrupted airflow to the engines regardless of the aircraft's angle of attack or velocity. The intakes themselves are S-shaped along their length. This design feature ensures that the engine turbine blades are not within frontal view of the intake, which in turn lowers the Typhoon's radar cross-section from the front. The intake box has a rounded bottom with sloping sides which improves airflow and further reduces

ABOVE Two 29 (R) Squadron twin-seat Typhoon FGR4s refuel from an RAF VC10 tanker aircraft while a Tornado GR4 stands off. Range is the Achilles heel of all fighter jets. Without refuelling, the Typhoon's endurance is a maximum of 90 minutes. *(RAF)*

RIGHT AND BELOW The internal S-shaped design of the Typhoon's chin-mounted air intake ensures the engine's turbine blades are not within frontal view. This lowers the Typhoon's radar cross-section from the front. In the lower picture can be seen the variable position lower cowl in its fully open position. *(RAF)*

the radar cross-section. The intake is fitted with a variable position lower cowl while the upper cowl is fixed.

The left-hand air intake has an ice detector fitted, which is one of the places that ice is most likely to form. The detector consists of a transducer, with a piece of metal that vibrates at a certain frequency. If ice forms, it will affect the frequency and it triggers a warning in the cockpit to alert the pilot so he can perform the necessary action.

Wing

The Typhoon has a delta wing. Delta wings are triangular in shape with the name's etymology rooted in the Greek alphabet. The fourth letter is 'delta', which in capital form is the shape of a triangle, hence the name.

Delta wings offer certain advantages over swept-wing designs. With a large enough angle of rearward sweep, a delta wing's leading edge will not contact the shock wave boundary formed at the nose of the fuselage as the speed of the aircraft approaches and exceeds transonic to supersonic velocity. The rearward sweep angle vastly lowers the airspeed normal to the leading edge of the wing, thereby allowing the aircraft to fly at high subsonic, transonic, or supersonic speed, while the over wing speed of the lifting air is kept to less than the speed of sound.

The delta form gives the largest total wing

LEFT The Typhoon's delta-wing is exceptionally strong to cope with the immense loads placed upon it in the high-G environment. Each wing could, in theory, support the weight of 35 Volkswagen Golf cars. *(Geoff Lee/ Eurofighter)*

area (generating useful lift) for the wing shape, with very low loading per unit of wing area, which permits high manoeuvrability in the airframe. As the delta's platform carries across the entire aircraft, it can be built much more strongly than a swept wing, where the spar meets the fuselage far in front of the centre of gravity. Generally a delta will be stronger than a similar swept wing, as well as having much more internal volume for fuel and other storage.

The Typhoon's wings are about as svelte as it's possible to make them but appearances can be deceptive. Thin and fragile as they appear, they're also immensely strong; they have to be, to cope with the immense G-forces that act on them. To put that in perspective, each wing could accommodate the weight of 35 Volkswagen Golfs. Automatic slats are present on the leading edges to ensure the correct wing camber is maintained across the flight envelope.

There is a 53° leading edge sweepback on the wing as this configuration offers the optimal combination of lift and agility. With an area of around 50 square metres, the wing has a small loading in typical combat situations which adds to the aircraft's exceptional manoeuvrability. Pitch instability causes the aircraft to point its nose up during flight, further increasing agility and helping to reduce drag.

Each wing is a multi-spar construction with integral fuel tanks. There are full-span inboard and outboard flaperons and leading edge slats, with wing tips housing the advanced defensive aid sub-system. The main undercarriage

BELOW This Typhoon is taxying at Gioia del Colle airbase in Italy during Operation Ellamy. Its foreplanes are deployed in airbrake (or lift dump) mode. Clearly visible in this image are the Paveway surface-to-ground munitions, which were used extensively. *(RAF)*

attachment is located on each wing. The wing's skin and spars are made from Carbon Fibre Composites (CFC), with the spars co-bonded to the lower skin. The ribs are carbon fibre reinforced, with metallic hard points. Titanium is used for the wing/fuselage attachments and outboard flaperons.

Foreplanes

These small front wings for the Typhoon (sometimes known as 'canards') are an essential component of the aircraft's strategic and tactical performance. Given the Typhoon's inherently unstable flight characteristic, it is only able to remain airborne due to flying attitude corrections being applied to the foreplanes via the onboard computers hundreds of times a second. The foreplanes both move independently of one another.

The foreplanes impart pitch and roll control when combined with the wing flaperons and rudder. They're used to trim the aircraft through different flight regimes thus minimising drag, and they can also be used as an extra pair of airbrakes when landing by pointing them straight down, thus *maximising* drag.

They are mounted much closer to the nose than is usual for fighter or multi-role jets. The effect of this is an increase in the maximum achievable angle of attack, although there is a compromise in terms of a decreased view to the left and right of the pilot.

Manufactured in titanium, the all-moving

foreplanes are superplastically formed and diffusion-bonded for minimum mass, high strength and optimum aerodynamic profile. These control surfaces provide the aircraft with high agility and instant responsiveness to the pilot's inputs. Acting as air-brakes, the foreplanes also help to reduce the aircraft's landing roll – the distance it needs to stop after touching down.

Undercarriage

'Three greens.' It's a mantra that most pilots recite in their heads as they deploy the main landing gear on approach, waiting milliseconds for the reassuring green glow that signifies that the aircraft's three wheels are down and locked into place.

The Typhoon's maximum permissible takeoff weight is 23,500kg. At the point of rotation (the moment of take-off) the main gear is loaded up as the aircraft's rear end squats and the nose wheel and front end lift off the runway. The

maximum landing weight is 18,800kg with a speed on approach of around 185 knots. The landing gear is primarily a shock absorber, its purpose to absorb and dissipate kinetic energy on touchdown.

The landing gear has to be able to cope with a wide spectrum of demands, given the Typhoon's ability to take off in just 300m and land on a strip just 700m long. The system used is a relatively standard tricycle type with a single wheel on each unit and tyres specially developed and manufactured by Dunlop.

The wing units retract inwards while the nose unit retracts backward. The main wheels measure 30.5in x 10in while the nose wheel measures 20in x 8.5in. Actual control of the nose wheel is handled as a secondary function by the Flight Control System. An emergency arrestor hook is fitted to the rear of the fuselage.

Retraction and extension of the Typhoon's landing gear is electrically signalled and hydraulically actuated. Normal deployment of the gear from selection via the lever to the down

ABOVE Each of the Typhoon's twin foreplanes moves independently of the other. They are controlled by the aircraft's on-board computers, which send out commands hundreds of times a second to keep the aircraft stable. *(RAF)*

RIGHT AND FAR RIGHT The Typhoon's undercarriage consists of a standard tricycle arrangement with a centre-wheel under the front fuselage and a wheel on each side under the wings. The wing units retract backwards, the nose wheel forwards. *(Author)*

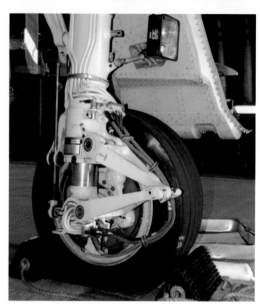

RIGHT AND FAR RIGHT The tyres on the Typhoon are specially manufactured by Dunlop. An undercarriage's principal job is to act as a shock-absorber, dissipating kinetic energy whenever the aircraft touches down. *(Author)*

RIGHT The pilot selects 'gear up' as this 3 (F) Squadron Typhoon takes off for a sortie over Libya during Operation Ellamy. Clearly visible in this image are the wing-mounted fuel drop tanks, added to increase the aircraft's endurance. *(RAF)*

and locked position takes about five seconds at +1G. In the event of a hydraulic malfunction, the pilot simply selects gear down using an emergency switch in the cockpit and the system is lowered via the secondary hydraulic system.

The brakes lead a miserable existence, working as they do at the extreme temperatures that high speed and heavy weight dictate. The discs on each wheel are carbon fibre, so they need to be hot to be effective – between 180°C and 300°C.

Fin

The fin and conventional rudder are manufactured from CFC with aluminium lithium on the leading and trailing edges, and GRP on the tip. As well as providing lateral stability, the fin also houses a number of key aircraft systems.

The structure is made of CFC, GRP, aluminium and titanium. These construction materials provide a rigid structure, whilst at the same time saving weight and enhancing the aircraft's aerodynamic performance.

Systems

Fuel

The Typhoon's main fuel storage tanks are located in the wings, with an additional spine tank just behind the cockpit, and two central tanks mounted in the fuselage. External tanks can be carried on three hard points (one

on each wing and one on the centreline position of the fuselage). The main fuel tanks hold 4,200 litres, whilst the wing tanks each have a capacity of 1,300 litres. The centreline drop tank holds 1,000 litres. Fully fuelled and carrying all three external tanks (a configuration normally only adopted for ferrying the aircraft over long distances), the Typhoon's range without air-to-air refuelling is approximately 870 miles.

As the aircraft manoeuvres in the air, fuel moves under gravity from one side of the plane to the other, with obvious consequences for the stability of the aircraft. To counteract these movements, pressure sensors spaced around the fuel tanks detect the difference in fuel levels within the tanks and feed back a signal to a control system. This control system then activates fuel

ABOVE The fin provides lateral stability. This 3 (F) Squadron Typhoon fin is painted in the squadron's commemorative anniversary paint scheme. *(RAF)*

LEFT A fuel drop tank is attached to the wing of this Typhoon as XI Squadron technicians prepare it for a sortie. Each wing tank has a capacity of 1,300 litres to extend the Typhoon's range. *(Author)*

valves which balance fuel distribution across the aircraft so as to constantly maintain the aircraft's centre of gravity.

Regulation, monitoring and control of the fuel system valves and pumps is handled automatically and the remaining fuel at any given time can be graphically displayed on any one of the pilot's cockpit screens.

Hydraulics

Hydraulics are essential to the integrity of any aircraft, but there are *eight* separate systems on the Typhoon that require a hydraulic supply. These consist of the flight control surface actuators; undercarriage; brakes; nose wheel steering system; air intake (moveable lower cowl) control; cockpit canopy; air-refuelling probe; and the Mauser BK27 cannon.

Loss of hydraulic power would obviously be catastrophic, rendering the flight control surfaces inoperable as well as preventing undercarriage deployment and retraction. The Typhoon includes two fully-redundant hydraulic systems pressurised to 4,000psi, each of which incorporate isolation valves so a failure in one of the other systems shouldn't lead to the loss of hydraulic power for the control surfaces. Both systems are powered by engine-driven gearboxes.

Adjustments are made to the flying control surfaces continually as the aircraft flies by the computer-controlled FCS system. This uses closed-loop control to adjust elevation according to pressure readings from four air data transducers, enabling the aircraft to perform advanced complex combat manoeuvres. These transducers communicate directly with the aircraft's flight control computers using a digital interface. As the transducers are used in a safety critical role, double or triple redundancy is built into the system.

Electrics

The Typhoon has two electrical systems, the primary power generation and distribution system and the secondary systems (including the auxiliary power unit). Primary power is supplied via the engine turbines through a LucasVarity/BAE Systems distribution and rectification system. Using this, electrical power can be supplied at a number of voltages and AC phases as well as supplying a DC output.

The DC system is fully redundant with two back-up rectifier units in case the two primaries fail. Additionally a DC battery source is available in emergencies as well as to power up the Auxiliary Power Unit (APU).

The secondary system provides a back-up using air-driven turbines in case of total or partial engine failure. Since the Typhoon is designed for autonomous operation the aircraft includes an APU as part of the secondary system. Before the engines are started the APU generates all the AC/DC power required to operate the aircraft's systems. The engine starting systems are also powered by the APU.

Air conditioning and pressurisation

The on-board systems of pressurisation, air conditioning and oxygen supply provides for the pilot's survival and reasonable comfort in what is effectively a hostile environment, as well as his capability to control the cockpit environment.

Although the cockpit is pressurised to maintain a cabin altitude of 16,000ft regardless of the actual altitude of the aircraft, it's vital that the pilot has an oxygen supply system in order to avoid loss of consciousness in case of rapid depressurisation due to fuselage damage. In the Typhoon, this oxygen system consists of a rubber breathing mask connected through a quick-coupling rubber hose to the oxygen flow piping and the oxygen supply source. Between the source and the breathing set, a regulator

OPPOSITE Hydraulics/ Flight Control Software (FCS) test. There are eight separate systems on the Typhoon that require a hydraulic supply. These are catered for by the Typhoon's two fully-redundant hydraulic systems. *(RAF)*

BELOW The cockpit is pressurised to maintain the cabin altitude below 16,000ft. At these cabin pressures there is not enough oxygen available to robustly maintain consciousness so each pilot wears an oxygen mask. Airliner cabins are pressurised to maintain the cabin altitude below 8,000ft. *(RAF)*

AIR PRESSURE AT ALTITUDE

Normal life is possible only up to an altitude of around 6,500ft – at higher altitudes human physiology is subjected to increasingly severe stresses that can only be corrected through a long acclimatisation period.

At 21%, the proportion of oxygen in the air remains almost unchanged up to 70,000ft. However, the actual air density – and therefore the number of molecules of oxygen in the air – drops as altitude increases. Consequently, the amount of oxygen available to sustain mental and physical alertness decreases markedly at altitudes above 10,000ft.

No permanent human habitation occurs above 18,000ft and beyond 26,000ft, no acclimatisation is feasible as life becomes practically impossible due to the onset of hypoxia, a condition caused by an insufficiency of oxygen in the blood. The symptoms of hypoxia depend on its severity and acceleration of onset. In the case of altitude sickness, where hypoxia develops gradually, the symptoms include headaches, fatigue, shortness of breath, and feelings of euphoria and nausea. In severe hypoxia, or in cases where the onset is rapid, loss of consciousness, pulmonary or cerebral embolism and eventually death usually occur.

BELOW The pilot can adjust the amount of pure oxygen delivered under pressure through his mask. On transit flights, the pilot can remove his mask for short periods to allow him to eat and drink. *(RAF)*

dilutes oxygen with the air present in the cabin, at concentrations of up to 100% oxygen, selected by the pilot.

The Typhoon's oxygen generation system is based on a molecular sieve fed by bleed air from the engines. This unit provides all the filtered air required and allows operation in situations where NBC (Nuclear, Biological, and Chemical) agents may be present. As the system uses engine bleed air, operation of the oxygen generator before engine start relies on the APU for its air supply.

In addition to supplying breathing air to the pilot, and to inflate the bladders in the pilot's anti-G suit, the Typhoon also provides for systems cooling and conditioning. For example the ECR-90, FLIR sensor and the conditioned anti-G suit must all be cooled. In addition the avionics bay systems require conditioning to maintain proper operation. To provide for this, liquid refrigerant systems are present with the Typhoon's fuel serving as the primary heat sink.

Flight Control System

However capable a single-seat fighter aircraft is, the ultimate objective is to free the pilot from flying it. The less the pilot has to do in terms of conventional flying, the more he is able to do in terms of using the aircraft to fight the enemy. Forget that it flies for a moment and look at it for what it really is – a weapons platform.

The Typhoon's foreplane/delta configuration is by nature aerodynamically unstable. The instability of the aircraft is derived from the position of a theoretical 'pressure point' on its longitudinal axis. This is calculated from the contribution to lift from each of the aircraft components (the wings, canards, fuselage etc). If the pressure point is in front of the centre of gravity on the longitudinal axis, the aircraft is aerodynamically unstable and it is impossible for a human to control it without computer assistance.

In subsonic flight the Typhoon's pressure

OPPOSITE The pilot of this Italian display Typhoon, fitted with smokewinders, applies max reheat as he tips the aircraft into a high-G turn. The flight control system ensures that regardless of control inputs, the aircraft never exceeds its maximum parameters. *(RAF)*

A 29 (R) Squadron display aircraft. The aircraft's flight envelope characteristics are pre-programmed to prevent the pilot from pushing the jet outside its stress/strain limits. *(RAF)*

point lies in front of the centre of gravity, therefore making the aircraft aerodynamically unstable. This is why the aircraft has such a complex Flight Control System – computers react quicker than a pilot. When the Typhoon crosses into supersonic flight the pressure point moves behind the centre of gravity, giving a stable aircraft. The advantages of an intentionally unstable design over that of a stable arrangement include greater agility – particularly at subsonic speeds – reduced drag, and an overall increase in lift (which also enhances STOL performance).

To achieve the Typhoon's extreme agility, it is designed so that without input to any control surfaces, the aircraft will rapidly pitch up during flight, necessitating a system that enables controlled flight to be maintained. This is achieved through a Fly-By-Wire (FBW) Flight Control System (FCS).

With this system the pilot has no direct link to any of the aircraft's control surfaces. Instead, all movements of the throttle, stick or pedals are interpreted by the FCS and an appropriate control response taken. There is no manual reversion in case of FCS failure and thus it must be extremely robust.

The FCS is a full-authority, quadruplex digital Fly-By-Wire system providing what

Eurofighter describes as 'full carefree handling and manoeuvring'. It is designed to enable the pilot to concentrate on the tactical tasks and to fly the aircraft 'head-up' in combination with the HOTAS (Hand-on Throttle and Stick) design. Emergency features have also been embodied in the system including low speed auto recovery, emergency 'G' over-ride, 'G' onset limitation, Dis-Orientation Recovery Capability (DORC) and automatic reversion.

The system is controlled by four Flight Control Computers and features primary and secondary actuation to ensure control along all axes (pitch, roll and yaw). The aerodynamic configuration is automatically trimmed to achieve an optimum compromise between performance and manoeuvrability.

Control surfaces are moved by the two independent hydraulic systems incorporated in the aircraft, which are powered by a 4000psi engine-driven gearbox. Pitch control is provided by symmetric operation of foreplanes and wing flaperons, while roll control is primarily achieved through differential operation of wing flaperons. Yaw control is primarily provided by the fin-mounted rudder. Cross feeds among the various actuation systems are also implemented to optimise aircraft performance and handling qualities. The slats and flaperons automatically optimise the wing camber at all angles of attack.

One of the benefits of the Typhoon's FCS is that the aircraft's flight envelope characteristics can be programmed directly into it, preventing the pilot from pushing the plane outside its stress/strain limits, for instance by pulling too sharp a climb or too tight a turn. Eurofighter terms this capability 'Carefree Handling' and it negates the need for pilots to constantly monitor their own flight actions. Similarly, the FCS can be programmed to compensate for external factors such as gusting, which can suddenly lead to loss of aircraft control.

The Typhoon's FCS is at all times aware of flight parameters such as speed, altitude, configuration, aircraft mass and balance, all of which define the prevailing structural and aerodynamic limits. In combat this provides two significant benefits. To get the utmost performance from the aircraft, the pilot often needs to fly at the highest possible G, or angle of attack, yet without exceeding aircraft limits.

TRIMMING AN AIRCRAFT

On conventional aircraft, trim tabs are small surfaces connected to the trailing edge of a larger control surface, used to adjust the trim of the controls. Their role is to counteract aerodynamic forces and stabilise the aircraft in a particular attitude, obviating the need for the pilot to constantly apply a control force. This is achieved by adjusting the angle of the tab relative to the larger surface.

As the desired position of a control surface changes, adjustable trim tabs allow the operator to reduce the manual force required to maintain that position – to zero, if used correctly. All aircraft must have a system for ensuring trim in the longitudinal axis, though methods other than trim tabs can be utilised – on many supersonic aircraft, fuel is shifted between tanks during the flight to avoid aerodynamic drag entirely.

On the Typhoon, all trim functions are completely automated and handled by the Flight Control System making a significant reduction to the pilot's workload during sustained manoeuvres, particularly when climbing or descending. This allows the pilot to focus attention on other critical tasks.

Additionally, the pilot is forced to monitor the aircraft instruments and make continuous, small adjustments in response to changing indications and to achieve best performance in combat. RAF pilots flying the Typhoon can quickly demand maximum performance from the aircraft, such as by pulling the control stick fully back, safe in the knowledge that the aircraft will respond with the maximum performance available without exceeding any of its limitations. The second benefit is that, because pilots do not need to worry about flying within the aircraft's limits, they can devote 100% of their attention to opponents, rather than monitoring aircraft parameters.

Autopilot

The Typhoon's autopilot is designed both for cruising, and to free the pilot in tactical situations. The autopilot provides basic track, heading, altitude and airspeed modes, and allows the pilot to fly optimum attack profiles automatically. The autopilot is an integrated part of the pilot's tactical control.

Automatic Recovery System

In the event of pilot disorientation, the Typhoon's FCS allows for rapid and automatic recovery by the simple press of a button. On selection of this auto-recovery facility the FCS takes full

LEFT The Disorientation Recovery Button is clearly marked and accessible to the pilot. In event of disorientation, the pilot can push this and the aircraft will return to a stabilised wings-level, gentle-climbing attitude. *(Author)*

control of the engines and flying controls, and automatically stabilises the aircraft in a wings level, gentle climbing attitude at 300 knots, until the pilot is ready to retake control.

Inside the cockpit

The Typhoon's cockpit is as advanced as it gets in terms of aircraft design. It is relatively roomy, with 360° horizontal visibility. It's an all-glass design without any conventional instruments – even for back up. Instead, it

LEFT Typhoon FGR4 cockpit. *(RAF)*

ABOVE In this view from the rear cockpit of a Typhoon T3 it is possible to appreciate the wide field of vision afforded to its crew. The Typhoon's cockpit is about as advanced as it gets in design terms. It is an all-glass design so there are no conventional instruments. The pilot relies on three full-colour multifunction displays. *(RAF)*

OPPOSITE The Typhoon's wide-angle, rimless, Head-Up Display (HUD) presents all relevant flight information to the pilot so he can maintain situational awareness at all times without having to look down. *(RAF)*

incorporates three full-colour Multifunction Head-Down Display screens (MHDDs), a wide-angle Head-Up Display (HUD) with Forward-Looking Infra-Red (FLIR), Voice, Throttle And Stick (VTAS), a Helmet-Mounted Symbology System (HMSS), a Multifunctional Information Distribution System (MIDS), a Manual Data-Entry Facility (MDEF) located on the left glareshield, and a fully integrated aircraft warning system with a Dedicated Warnings Panel (DWP). Reversionary flying instruments, lit by LEDs, are located under a hinged right glareshield.

The needs of the single-seat pilot have been paramount at all stages of the cockpit's design process. High workload situations were analysed to establish priorities such as those required for head-in and head-out operations. Displays and moding have been designed so that only necessary information is presented to the pilot.

The instrumentation is minimal, presented on the three MHDD screens which are configurable by the pilot to display only the most relevant information at any given time. The Helmet-Mounted Display (HMD) provides the pilot with all the tactical information he needs for all stages of his mission. Cockpit lighting is compatible with night vision enhancement, and daytime brightness of the displays is automatically adjusted. VTAS technology gives optimum intuitive controls and enhances the efficiency of the single seat operation. From his complex, snug-fitting Martin-Baker Mk 16a Ejector seat, the pilot flies and fights the aircraft, using all the controls and systems available to him.

This automation is enhanced through the Attack and Identification System, which fuses all of the available sensor (both on-board and off-board) data thus reducing the pilot's need to cross-check information.

Head-Up Display (HUD)

The Typhoon's advanced wide-angle (35° by 25°) HUD is arguably the single greatest improvement in cockpit design since the first fighter was flown. Like all similar systems it utilises an angled semi-reflective screen directly in the pilot's view through the forward canopy.

RIGHT Keypad entry system and gear select lever. *(Author)*

RIGHT Cockpit left-hand side showing gear handle, camera and seat oxygen. *(Author)*

FAR RIGHT Reversionary flying instruments, with hinged glareshield open. *(Author)*

BELOW Cockpit right-hand side showing seat safe egress. *(Author)*

BELOW RIGHT Rudder pedal – left. *(Author)*

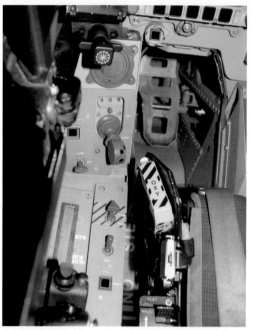

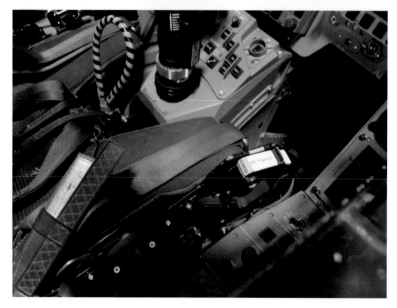

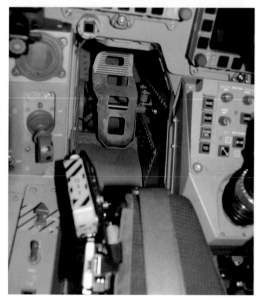

The unit is frameless which, in turn, reduces problems with visibility in the frontal hemisphere.

HUD is able to display the full range of flight parameters, from basic flight information such as altitude, speed, heading and weapons mode through to specific targeting and systems information. The navigation system can project terrain-following cues, and the weapons mode displays specific HUD symbols. A free-fall weapon for example would display a continuously computed impact point, whereas an air-to-air missile would display a tracking diamond.

Directly below the HUD is a 24-line, 10-column LED display that outputs various mission and system-critical data. Other LED displays present information such as the selected radio channel, and left and right engine fuel. The HUD also incorporates the cockpit audio/video recording facilities.

Multifunction Head-Down Display (MHDD)

The three full-colour MHDDs present a wide range of information to the pilot, including the overall tactical situation, attack formats, weapons information, radar and map displays, air traffic procedures, system status and check lists. All of the available formats can be shown on any of the three MHDDs, with detailed information selected with either the multi-function soft keys arranged around each display, an X/Y cursor control located on the joystick, or by DVI (Direct Voice Input).

The displays utilise a quad-green pixel system which allows them to output full-colour images (including full-motion video) and high-resolution monochrome images from the Typhoon's FLIR (Forward-Looking Infra-Red). A standard set-up is generally defined for each monitor, which is then selected automatically by the Typhoon's systems as appropriate for the current mission or situation.

ABOVE The three cockpit MHDDs are fully configurable by each pilot to display the most pertinent information, from a moving map display to armaments and fuel flow. *(Author)*

RIGHT The BAE Striker helmet enables the pilot to cue the Typhoon's sensors and weapons onto enemy aircraft simply by looking at it. *(RAF)*

BAE Striker Helmet and Helmet Mounted Display (HMD)

The Striker's Helmet-Mounted Display (HMD) is one of the most complex avionics systems in the world, providing flight reference data and weapon aiming through the pilot's visor. Like the aircraft's Head-Up Display, it also provides the pilot with aircraft information without the need to look inside the cockpit. In the case of the HMD this 'head out' advantage is retained wherever the pilot is looking, rather than fixed to the forward view, as with the HUD.

This means that the Typhoon pilot can direct a missile to look in the direction of a

target and the missile can then be locked on to it. The pilot can maintain the target visually even at angular extremes such as the elusive 'over the shoulder' shot, thus providing a true 'look and shoot' capability.

Hand-On Throttle & Stick (HOTAS)

Key to the level of integration and automation seen in the cockpit is the combination of Direct Voice Input (DVI) and Hand-On Throttle And Stick (HOTAS). Combined, these systems are known as Voice, Throttle And Stick (VTAS).

HOTAS controls allow the pilot to carry out complex tasks with relative ease during intense situations by incorporating 24 programmable buttons on the throttle and stick (12 on each). These buttons can be programmed to handle functions relating to both defence and offence. These include the switching of Defensive Aids Sub-System (DASS) modes, weapon systems, target manipulation, and return to level flight. In addition the control column incorporates a pointer device for moving a cursor around each of the MHDDs.

ABOVE Throttle with programmable buttons. *(Author)*

LEFT Stick with programmable buttons. *(Author)*

Sensor fusion

The Typhoon's avionics and sensors suite is one of its greatest assets, giving the pilot the edge in high mission effectiveness and survivability in high-threat situations.

Sensor fusion is the term for the processing of information received and transmitted by the key aircraft sensors. This information is presented to the pilot clearly and accurately, in an uncluttered fashion, to allow for safe and efficient single-seat operation in the swing-role environment. The high level of integration and sharing of information between the various sub-systems gives the pilot an autonomous ability to assess rapidly the overall tactical situation and respond efficiently to identified threats.

Radar

The CAPTOR Mechanical Scan Radar is the best performing type of its class. This multi-mode pulse-Doppler radar is the first airborne radar in NATO with three as opposed to two processing channels. The third channel is used in a jamming scenario. The radar provides air-to-air and air-to-surface features.

Infra-Red

The CAPTOR is an active system, which operates by transmitting radio waves and detecting the returning waves which have bounced off other airborne objects. Whenever the radar is operational the power it outputs can be detected by an enemy using a Radar Warning Receiver (RWR). To avoid this, an alternative method is to use an on-board passive system. The Passive Infra-Red Airborne Tracking Equipment (PIRATE) is a second-generation Imaging Infra-Red (IIR) system which uses passive detection in a frequency band complementary to that of the radar. Passive air-to-air target detection and tracking performance in the IRST mode provides totally covert tracking capabilities. The system itself utilises a highly sensitive infra-red sensor mounted on the port side of the canopy.

PIRATE also fully supports air-to-surface operations in the Forward-Looking Infra-Red mode, with ground and target imagery as required during missions where passive operations are also needed. PIRATE allows the

detection of both the hot exhaust plumes of jet engines as well as surface heating caused by friction. By supercooling the sensor, even small variations in temperature can be detected at long range. PIRATE gives a high-resolution image of targets which can be directed to any of the cockpit's MHDDs, as well as overlaid on both the Helmet-Mounted Sight and Head-Up Display.

Multifunctional Information Distribution System (MIDS)

The MIDS is a high-capacity digital information distribution system allowing the secure, jam-resistant sharing of real-time data between a wide variety of users, including all the components of a tactical air force, and where appropriate, land and naval forces. Using this command and control system, a Typhoon's pilot can listen to, and see, all relevant data on friendly and enemy forces, airfields, command decisions or mission changes, all over huge ranges and in any direction. The Typhoon has the capacity to absorb all of this information and process it via the sensor fusion capability to present a clear and relevant battle space picture to the pilot.

The system presents a comprehensive tactical environment on the MHDDs, relieving the pilot of the need to assemble the necessary information from a large number of independent sources. It also ensures the pilot is aware of threat and friendly aircraft which are beyond the areas covered by Radar and Infra-Red Search and Track (IRST).

Electro-Optic (EO) Targeting System

Autonomous operations are enhanced by the addition of on-board target detection, recognition and identification, using the latest EO sensor technology. This is complemented by on-board laser tracking supporting target designation for self or third-party operations.

Navigation

The Typhoon assists pilot workload with a highly advanced autopilot that incorporates attitude hold functionality.

Navigational awareness is obtained via a Global Positioning System (GPS) and backed

OPPOSITE **Head-on view showing the PIRATE Sensor.** *(RAF)*

up with an Inertial Navigation System (INS). Although GPS is now the de-facto standard, INS is arguably the best aircraft navigation system ever produced. Forged in the crucible of the Apollo moon-shot programme, it is a self-contained, accurate, reliable world-wide navigation system that works using a triple-gyro set and electronics that measure the smallest of accelerations. From the acceleration readings speed is calculated, and from speed, distance with time. The INS provides output via the flight instruments as well as providing navigation guidance to the autopilot.

Landing aids are provided by an Instrumented Landing System (ILS) and Microwave Landing System (MLS) and Differential Global Navigation Satellite System (DGNSS) operation. The Typhoon's navigation system is Electronic Counter Measure (ECM) resistant.

Praetorian – the Defensive Aids Sub-System (DASS)

Typhoon employs a sophisticated and highly integrated Defensive Aids Sub-System (DASS) named Praetorian, which monitors and responds automatically to all air-to-air and air-to-surface threats. It provides an all-round prioritised assessment, and can respond to multiple threats simultaneously. Threat detection methods include a Radar Warning Receiver (RWR) and a Laser Warning Receiver (LWR). Protection is provided by chaff and flares dispensers, Electronic Counter Measures (ECM) and a supersonically-capable Towed Radar Decoy (TRD).

Praetorian provides complete 360° spherical detection and protection capabilities, making it one of the most advanced self-protection systems available. It monitors and responds to the outside world and consists of a number of systems to detect threats, including a Radar Warning Receiver (RWR). Radar is one of the fundamental sensors available on modern fighter jets, but its use also puts an aircraft at risk since, as an active system, it emits electromagnetic radiation. The Typhoon's RWR is designed to detect these emissions, providing the pilot with not just a bearing, but also the likely type of radar and the platform it's deployed on.

Any fighter pilot aims to remove an enemy aggressor before they have fired. Clearly, this isn't always possible so Praetorian also incorporates three antennae that alert the Missile Approach Warner (MAW) – one each near the cockpit in the port and starboard wing roots, and one in the rear of the fuselage near the tail. Its effectiveness is enhanced by the system being linked to the Typhoon's flare launchers, giving an instantaneous response to any threat.

As most aircraft are fitted with laser range-finding equipment to accurately determine distances, there are also laser-guided weapons available which ride the beam to their target. Praetorian counters these threats with its Laser Warning Receiver. The units detect any incoming laser radiation and determine its bearing.

Alongside its set of dedicated sensor systems to detect any threats to the Typhoon, Praetorian also incorporates a full range of counter measures, which can be automatically engaged as required (although the pilot can also utilise them at will via the VTAS system).

Chaff remains one of the fundamental defences available to fighter aircraft. The Typhoon's chaff dispensers are carried inside the outer wing pylons, thus freeing the pylons for the carriage of weapons. The system can be controlled automatically by Praetorian, or manually by the pilot.

ABOVE Starboard side wingtip DASS pod with Tower Radar Decoy apertures. *(Author)*

BELOW Chaff dispenser under wing. *(Author)*

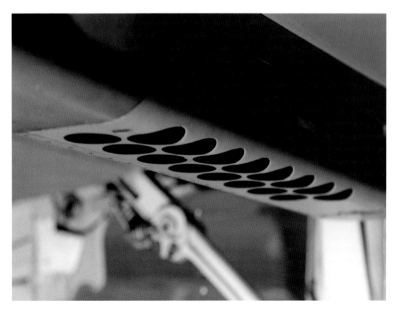

Pyrotechnic flares were a simple yet effective counter to the development of infra-red guided weapons and are still a potent defence. As with chaff, the Typhoon's Praetorian includes flare launchers carried internally within the inboard wing fairings. They can be fired in a number of ways: manually by the pilot, automatically by the DASS and, in response to an immediate threat, by the MAWs. The release pattern is controlled automatically to minimise the risk of the incoming missile recognising the flares for what they are.

In addition, Electronic Counter Measures (ECM) are an integral part of Praetorian, emitting radio frequency energy directed at the threat. The ECM aims to either fool the opposing radar into thinking the aircraft is somewhere else or to overpower it completely thus rendering it useless. The ECM automatically activates the most suitable on or off-board counter to whatever threat is perceived while the information is simultaneously displayed graphically to the pilot via the cockpit's MHDDs. This allows the pilot the further options of manoeuvre or in some cases, manual override.

The radio frequency jammer is capable of decoying and jamming all types of radars such as Continuous Wave (CW), Pulse and Pulse-Doppler. The form of ECM generated can be altered by the DAC (Defensive Aids Computer) as required.

A Towed Radar Decoy is part of the Praetorian arsenal and is deployed on a Kevlar cable containing a fibre optic link and a separate power distribution line. The TRD is towed behind the aircraft and lures enemy missiles away by providing a much larger radar cross-section than the aircraft. It also incorporates the latest jamming techniques. Through the cable the DASS communicates with the TRD to transmit specific deception techniques from the threat library to defeat incoming missiles and hostile radars.

Space and computing power expansions will allow continuous evolution against future threats, enhance Eurofighter Typhoon's survivability and greatly increase overall mission effectiveness. The aircraft's design complements the DASS by minimising the Typhoon's radar and infra-red signature.

Banging out

Crew escape and life support

The RAF's Typhoon pilots normally access and exit the cockpit via either an external or integral ladder. The latter, designed for autonomous operations, is a telescopic arrangement stowed in the port side of the fuselage below the cockpit entry, and exit is through a combination of the ladder, foot rests and handholds.

Emergency escape is by the Martin Baker Mk 16a ejection seat.

No pilot ever *wants* to eject – ejecting is a last-resort solution which almost always involves the loss of the aircraft, and places the pilot's body under incredible stress. The system can be best understood by looking at one relatively recent ejection in detail.

Wednesday, 11 June 2003 is a date that will stay indelibly marked in the mind of Lieutenant Commander (Lt Cdr) Robert Schwab, a British Royal Navy Sea Harrier pilot. On a routine sortie whilst flying at 28,000ft over the coast of Devon, his Sea Harrier FA2 became uncontrollable and entered a spin. As the aircraft lost altitude, plunging 18,000ft and still spinning, Schwab reached between his legs and grabbed the ejection handle of his aircraft's Martin-Baker Mk 10h ejection seat.

There's an almost imperceptible delay when any fighter pilot takes the decision to eject and pulls the handle – where time becomes elastic and a stressed mind senses nothing happening. The reality is somewhat different as within two-tenths of a second after firing, the automated

BELOW Flt Lt Adam Crickmore with ejection seat in situ. *(Author)*

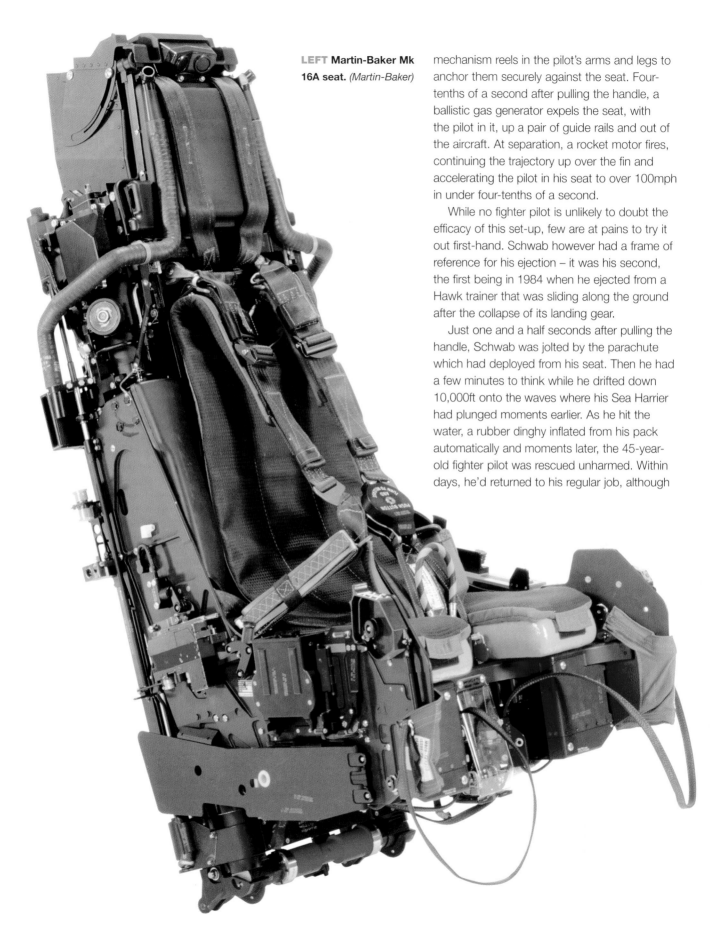

LEFT Martin-Baker Mk 16A seat. *(Martin-Baker)*

mechanism reels in the pilot's arms and legs to anchor them securely against the seat. Four-tenths of a second after pulling the handle, a ballistic gas generator expels the seat, with the pilot in it, up a pair of guide rails and out of the aircraft. At separation, a rocket motor fires, continuing the trajectory up over the fin and accelerating the pilot in his seat to over 100mph in under four-tenths of a second.

While no fighter pilot is unlikely to doubt the efficacy of this set-up, few are at pains to try it out first-hand. Schwab however had a frame of reference for his ejection – it was his second, the first being in 1984 when he ejected from a Hawk trainer that was sliding along the ground after the collapse of its landing gear.

Just one and a half seconds after pulling the handle, Schwab was jolted by the parachute which had deployed from his seat. Then he had a few minutes to think while he drifted down 10,000ft onto the waves where his Sea Harrier had plunged moments earlier. As he hit the water, a rubber dinghy inflated from his pack automatically and moments later, the 45-year-old fighter pilot was rescued unharmed. Within days, he'd returned to his regular job, although

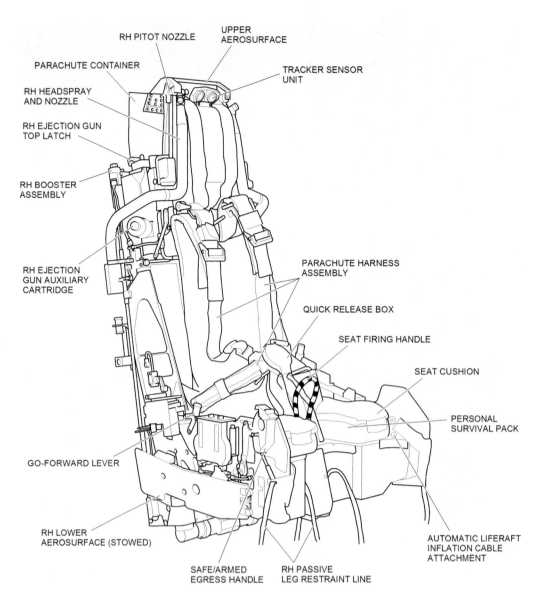

RH PITOT NOZZLE

UPPER AEROSURFACE

PARACHUTE CONTAINER

TRACKER SENSOR UNIT

RH HEADSPRAY AND NOZZLE

RH EJECTION GUN TOP LATCH

RH BOOSTER ASSEMBLY

RH EJECTION GUN AUXILIARY CARTRIDGE

PARACHUTE HARNESS ASSEMBLY

QUICK RELEASE BOX

SEAT FIRING HANDLE

SEAT CUSHION

PERSONAL SURVIVAL PACK

GO-FORWARD LEVER

RH LOWER AEROSURFACE (STOWED)

AUTOMATIC LIFERAFT INFLATION CABLE ATTACHMENT

SAFE/ARMED EGRESS HANDLE

RH PASSIVE LEG RESTRAINT LINE

his unit's doctor had suggested that he might refrain from ejector seats – and further back aggravation – for 90 days.

Even whilst Schwab was readjusting his mindset to having been flung from the relatively benign and stable environment of the cockpit into the maelstrom of noise and speed that is the airstream, a momentous milestone had been reached for the ejector seat's manufacturers, Martin Baker. With his expulsion from his aircraft, Lt Cdr Schwab's became the 7,000th life to be saved in over 60 years of building ejector seats. As of August 2012, that number had risen to 7,400. Everything's relative of course but by any yardstick, this is no small number. When each of those units represents a life, it becomes all the more remarkable.

The Typhoon's Martin Baker Mk 16a ejector seat is, as of 2012, the most advanced, sophisticated seat of its kind in production. As with the Typhoon itself, the seat is constructed of light alloys and advanced composite materials such as carbon fibre, and it has many advantages over previous seats. The simplified combined harness allows unassisted strap-in, and the passive leg restraint system avoids the need for the pilot to wear restraining garters. A second generation electronic sequencer is incorporated.

Reliability and maintainability are key elements of the design, with full access to in-cockpit components. The seat offers a high level of comfort and incorporates all the electrical and liquid/gas connections required between the pilot and his aircraft. It is integrated with the on-board primary oxygen supply, communication links, anti-g pressure supply, Nuclear Biological and Chemical (NBC) defence and communication systems, together with interfaces for the helmet-mounted systems. The narrow head box contributes to the Typhoon's excellent all-round vision. All these links are automatically severed and sealed upon an ejection sequence start. Following ejection the seat provides a 30-minute emergency oxygen supply (which would also automatically activate and deactivate upon primary oxygen failure or reinstatement within the cockpit). Additionally the seat incorporates its own auxiliary pressure suit feed reservoirs ensuring the pilot remains comfortable at high altitude.

Pilot workload in terms of the number of actions required to initiate egress is lower on the Mk16a than on any other ejection seat. All a pilot needs to do to eject is pull the firing handle; everything else from the canopy being jettisoned to the pilot being on a parachute is fully automatic and computer controlled.

In most ejection systems the ejection gun (the apparatus which propels the seat from the aircraft) consists of an explosive charge which when ignited burns instantaneously, propelling the seat at high speed (and high-G) from the aircraft. The Mk 16 however features a solid rocket type propellant which accelerates the seat in a more linear profile, reducing the high-G loads exerted on the pilot. The system also allows automatic adaptation to different pilot weights and distributions; the simplified version of the Typhoon's seat, the Mk 16l, allows for pilot weights from just 47kg to 111kg to be safely encompassed.

Once clear of the aircraft (a process taking around 0.46 seconds from the pilot pulling the ejection handle) the rocket motor sequence is initiated. The rockets themselves are designed for a fast burn cycle of around 0.25s while generating an instantaneous force of 20kN. The rocket assembly is designed to roll the chair to one side upon leaving the aircraft to enable safe chute deployment. This is achieved by over sizing one of the two nozzles fitted within the chair's base. In the two-seat Typhoon each seat is designed to roll in opposite directions to ensure safe ejection for both crew members.

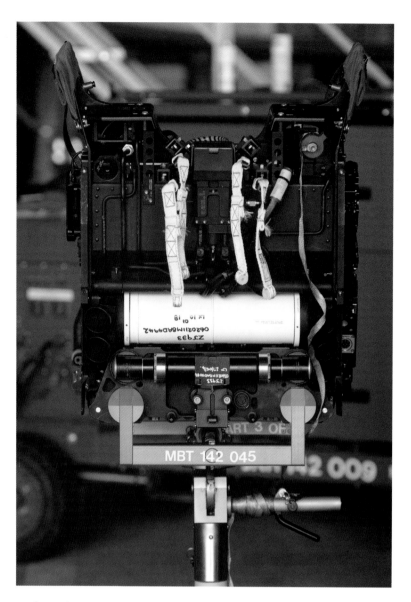

Once the seat has been propelled clear of the cockpit, a rocket motor is fired to lift the seat clear of the aircraft and aerodynamic surfaces are deployed for stability. At this point the seat's technology comes to the fore. Airspeed measuring devices are deployed and the airspeed and altitude are fed to a digital microprocessor together with the accelerations that the seat is experiencing. The computer then determines the safest sequence of timing of events to place the pilot on the parachute, all within milliseconds.

Travelling at 600 knots at sea level the pilot would be on the parachute within 1.8 seconds of pulling the ejection handle. In low-speed/low-altitude ejections the pilot's parachute is deployed within 0.27 seconds of pulling the handle.

ABOVE Underside detail of the Mk 16A seat. *(Author)*

Chapter Three

The Typhoon's beating heart

The EuroJet EJ200

The twin EuroJet EJ200 turbofan engines can propel the Typhoon to an altitude of 40,000ft within 90 seconds of 'brakes off'. With full reheat engaged the sheer power generated by the engines is unrivalled at a breathtaking 40,000lb of thrust. Without reheat they can still produce 28,000lb of thrust, enough to power the Typhoon to supersonic speeds.

OPPOSITE Max reheat on a damp day at RAF Coningsby. (Author)

Before we look at the engine that powers the Typhoon, let's go back to basics for a moment. All jet engines work on the principle of Sir Isaac Newton's third law of motion which states that for every action there is an equal and opposite reaction. In its simplest terms, this law can be demonstrated by releasing an inflated balloon. As the air escapes, it propels the balloon in the opposite direction. A jet engine produces the same effect.

Air enters the front intake of the jet engine and is compressed, then forced into combustion chambers. Fuel is sprayed into it and the mixture is ignited causing the gases that form to expand rapidly. They are then exhausted through the rear of the combustion chambers, exerting equal force in all directions and providing forward thrust as they escape. As the gases leave the engine, they pass through a turbine (a fan-like set of blades) rotating the turbine shaft. This shaft, in turn, rotates the compressor, thereby bringing in a fresh supply of air through the intake. Thrust can be increased by the afterburner section, or 'reheat,' whereby extra fuel is sprayed into the exhaust gases which then burn to give additional thrust. That's the science bit.

The sheer power generated by the Typhoon's twin EuroJet EJ200 jet engines is unrivalled. They are capable of propelling the aircraft to an altitude of 40,000ft within 90 seconds of 'brakes off'. With full reheat engaged, they produce an astonishing 40,000lb of thrust. On dry power – without reheat – they still produce 28,000lb of thrust, which is enough power to propel the Typhoon to supersonic speeds. Once

BELOW Brakes off to 40,000ft in 90 seconds. *(RAF)*

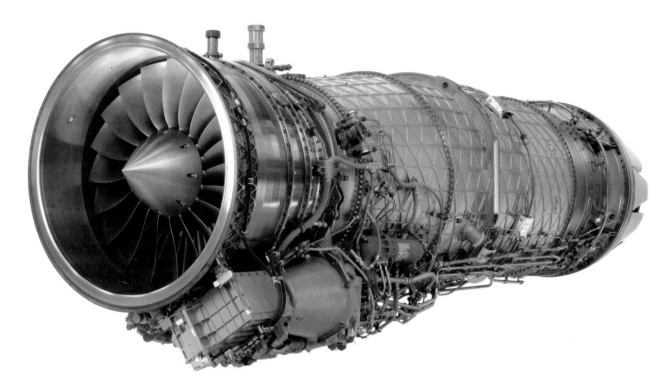

it reaches Mach 1, the Typhoon can maintain supersonic speed without reheat too, the so-called 'supercruise'. At sea level and with reheat engaged, the Typhoon can reach Mach 1 from 200 knots in just 30 seconds. The EJ200s are capable of generating a further 15% of dry thrust (a total of 31,050lb combined) and 5% reheat output (a total of 42,526lb combined) in a so-called 'war setting'. However, utilising this capability reduces the engines' life expectancy.

The engines' power on a max reheat take-off means that as it climbs, the Typhoon isn't really flying at all, at least not in accordance with the basic rules of flight. The delta wing provides lift at the point of rotation but, after that, the pilot simply pulls back on the stick and flies straight up so lift becomes an irrelevance. In essence, the Typhoon becomes a rocket, propelled to altitude on a cushion of its own power.

The twin EJ200s give the Typhoon the ability to fly at Mach 2.0. They mean the aircraft needs only a shade over 2,000ft of runway to get airborne and it can do so just eight seconds after brakes off. They give the pilot enough power that performing certain manoeuvres will expose him to G-forces from plus-9 to minus-3, and if necessary, take him to a ceiling of 60,000ft; in aviation, speed is life, altitude is life insurance.

Overview

EUROJET Turbo GmbH (EUROJET) is the management company responsible for the EJ200 engine system. The company's shareholders comprise Rolls-Royce (UK), Avio (Italy), ITP (Spain) and MTU Aero Engines (Germany). The company's responsibilities include the management of the development, support and export of the EJ200 powerplant, operating out of its headquarters in Hallbergmoos, Germany (near Munich airport).

The EJ200 started life in 1982 as the Rolls-Royce/MoD XG-40 Advanced Core Military Engine or ACME demonstrator. This programme, which ran until 1995, developed new fan, compressor, combustor, turbine (including high-temperature life prediction) and augmenter systems using advanced materials and new manufacturing processes. The first full engine commenced rig testing in December 1986 with the final XG-40 running for some 200 hours during 4,000 cycles, bringing the programme to a close in June 1995.

Upon formation of the EuroJet consortium in 1986 much of the continuing XG-40 research formed the basis of the new programme. The requirements were for a powerplant capable of higher thrust, longer life and lower complexity

ABOVE The Typhoon's EuroJet EJ200 powerplant is designed for a life of 6,000 flying hours – approximately 30 years of operation. *(EuroJet)*

than previous engines. The result was an engine with similar dimensions to the Tornado's RB199 yet having almost half as many parts (1,800 against 2,845 for the RB199) and delivering nearly 50% more thrust.

The EJ200 was deliberately developed with maintainability in mind. The rationale adopted by the design team was to ensure operational capability by keeping the engine 'on wing' for as long as possible. Experience from earlier generation engine programmes showed that when an engine is removed from the aircraft, significant costs are incurred. Such costs are based on the need to supply a serviceable spare engine for continued operation and also due to the inevitable scope creep that occurs during repair and overhaul of the removed engine. To maximise the 'on wing' duration of the EJ200, there was a conscious decision to increase component life, increase levels of reliability and to provide a 'no surprises' approach to engine management through intelligent Engine Health Monitoring (EHM)

The EJ200's Hot Gas Path Parts (HGPP) have been designed and manufactured to

ensure an extremely long life. The lives of the HGPP were purposely synchronised with the lives of other engine components meaning that the number of engine removals through an engine's life is reduced to the minimum.

As a further benefit, the EJ200 Mk101 follows an 'on condition' maintenance philosophy. This means that components are not simply replaced once a set number of engine hours are reached. Instead, they are monitored and replaced when their physical condition is deemed to be unacceptable or when the EHM system calculates a life and/or limit exceedance.

One of the EHM system's strengths is that it was designed as an 'end-to-end' system, fully integrated within the Typhoon airframe. This results in an unimpeded flow of validated data from the engine through to the operations centre. It is also possible to view EHM data whilst the aircraft is standing on the apron via the Maintenance Data Panel (MDP).

Through intelligent interpretation of the engine data, the EHM system is capable of monitoring each engine's operational

OPPOSITE EJ200 during manufacture. *(EuroJet)*

BELOW Maintenance of an EJ200 engine at RAF Coningsby's maintenance facility. The RAF's EuroJet EJ200 engines are assembled by Rolls-Royce in Bristol. *(Geoff Lee/Eurofighter)*

supersedes that of its competitors, delivering a high thrust-to-weight ratio with simple engine architecture. It is a two-spool turbo-based fan with modular design. The wide-chord fan with integrally bladed discs (blisks) is light and aerodynamically efficient and possesses high levels of resistance to Foreign Object Damage (FOD). The advanced aerodynamics employed in the fan allows optimum operation without the need for inlet guide vanes.

Both the three-stage low-pressure compressor and five-stage high-pressure compressor are driven by single-stage advanced air-cooled turbines, which utilise the latest single-crystal blade technology, operating at temperatures which are 300°C above those of previous generation engines. Engine brush seals are widely used rather than labyrinth seals in the air system. The annular combustor, incorporating air spray fuel injectors, has been designed for extremely low smoke and emission levels. The reheat system features radial hot stream burners, independent cold stream burning and the engine features a hydraulically operated convergent/divergent nozzle.

All accessories, including the Digital Engine Control and Monitoring Unit (DECMU), are self-contained and engine-mounted. The gearbox provides drive for accessories. The engine is designed for a life of 6,000 flying hours which corresponds to approximately 30 years of operation.

performance both on the ground and in-flight. This provides the RAF's engineers with a real-time account of component life usage and also a prognosis of future engine functional and mechanical performance. Having easy access to this level of data for each engine at the end of each sortie is key, particularly when taking executive decisions such as whether to deploy an engine or to remove it for maintenance.

The EJ200's advanced technology

Low-pressure (LP) compressor

The LP compressor is a three-stage, FOD-tolerant axial flow unit with a very high pressure-ratio (4.2:1). It is an all-blisk (integrally bladed disc) design featuring wide chord aerofoils attached by advanced linear friction welding techniques and operates without the need for inlet guide vanes.

High-pressure (HP) compressor

The axial flow HP compressor consists of five stages, delivering a pressure increase of 6.2:1 (overall the EJ200 compression system delivers 26:1 in only eight stages) with a high surge margin and only one set of variable inlet guide vanes.

Combustion system

The annular combustor is a very compact design employing the latest technology to achieve

RIGHT **An RAF technician performs routine maintenance on an EJ200 at RAF Coningsby. To protect the low-pressure compressor blades and the engine from damage when not in use the red panel is inserted into the intake mouth.** *(Geoff Lee/Eurofighter)*

extremely demanding requirements in terms of emissions (zero visible smoke), combustion stability/handling, efficiency and life. Features include advanced air spray fuel injectors with preferential fuelling, film cooling and thermal barrier coating and full boroscope access.

High-pressure (HP) turbine

The HP turbine is a single-stage, shroudless design using 3D, single-crystal, nickel alloy aerofoils with advanced internal and film cooling, ensuring long life, low blade numbers and high performance. Tip clearance control is also employed to maintain efficiency. The turbine blade temperature is measured by using an optical pyrometer, linked to the DECMU. Plasma-sprayed thermal barrier coatings are used on liners and vanes.

Low-pressure (LP) turbine

The LP turbine is a single-stage, shrouded design chosen for its high efficiency and performance retention characteristics. Single-crystal, cooled turbine blades are used in the turbine rotor and thermal barrier coatings are

BELOW **EJ200 cutaway drawing.** *(EuroJet)*

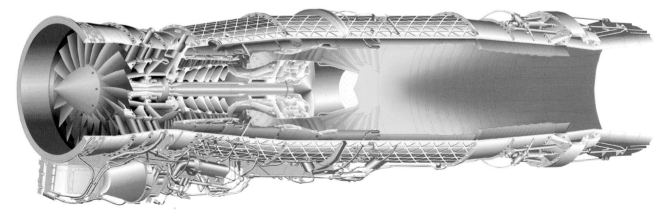

used on static components such as vanes. As with the HP turbine, this represents a step change from previous designs.

Reheat system

The advanced-staged afterburner system with radial burners and primary vaporisers in the hot stream and fuel injection in the cold stream gives very high combustion efficiency over the operational range. The three burners are independently supplied with fuel, giving continuous and smooth modulation between minimum and maximum reheat. The design achieves smooth selection and low smoke and maximum thrust boost whilst minimising instabilities.

Gearbox and oil system

The EJ200's gearbox is externally-sited and consists of a wrap-around design, positioned on the engine's underside for easy accessibility. It is a fully aerobatic, self-contained oil system with automatic oil debris monitoring. The oil tank is mounted on the front left side of the gearbox and contains a rotating basket which generates an artificial gravitational force thus ensuring a supply of oil to the pump, even under the most extreme flight manoeuvres.

Brush seals

Extensive use of brush seals is made throughout the engine; these have advantages in terms of reduced leakage, mass, lower heat transfer to oil and improved supportability.

Digital Engine Control and Monitoring Unit (DECMU)

The engine-mounted DECMU is a twin-lane, fault-tolerant system linked to the aircraft flight control system. It constantly monitors the functional status of the engine and allows precise, responsive and safe control at all times. The engine health monitoring system includes features such as individual component life usage, continuous vibration and oil debris monitoring, and event reporting. The whole engine is designed for on-condition maintenance and low life-cycle costs as supported by this technology.

Variable exhaust nozzle

The EJ200 features a convergent-divergent variable exhaust nozzle, optimised for multi-role, subsonic and supersonic performance. The nozzle position is controlled by the DECMU and is adjusted (modulated) constantly throughout the dry and wet range of operation.

Built-in growth potential

The EJ200 has been designed with built-in growth potential of up to 15%. Enhancements in the compression system and the latest

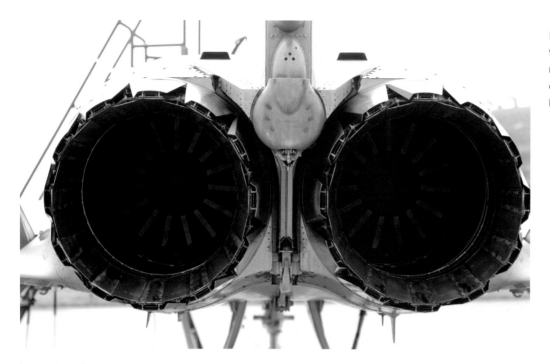

innovations in core engine technology could deliver up to 30% increased power. This performance improvement might also be traded for life-cycle cost improvements, maintaining current thrust levels. This flexibility is enabled by the advanced DECMU, fully exploiting the advantages of the enhanced engine in line with operational requirements.

Chapter Four

Licensed to kill

Mission profiles and weapons fit

The Typhoon's extensive multi-role/swing-role capability means it is capable of combining different operational tasks in a single mission. Armed with air-to-air and air-to-surface weapons it means that the Typhoon is able to switch roles in-flight – from air superiority to air interdiction to close air support – making it a highly effective swing-role weapon system.

OPPOSITE A fully loaded Typhoon undergoes flight-testing. Three drop tanks are usually only fitted for long-distance transit flights and never with a full complement of ordnance. *(Eurofighter)*

In the rapidly evolving nature of modern warfare, there is one capability requirement that remains constant above all others – that of air superiority. It is the speed and certainty by which air superiority can be established in a battle environment that determines how quickly and safely other operational tasks can be met.

As the world's most advanced multi-role combat aircraft, the Eurofighter Typhoon is the RAF's best bet to achieve air superiority and counter effectively all current and evolving threats. Air combat can be broken down into two broad categories: Beyond Visual Range (BVR) and Close In Combat (CIC).

The key to success in the BVR environment lies in a fighter aircraft achieving three firsts: first sight, first shot, and first kill. To achieve this, it helps if a fighter aircraft has every capability that its pilot might need to call on to get an edge over his opponent.

A typical BVR engagement utilising Typhoon would involve the positive identification of targets over 70 miles away, using the CAPTOR radar and data link systems to automatically assess and prioritise the threat. The Typhoon's pilot will then use the significant excess power of its two EJ200 engines to accelerate to around Mach 1.8, to close in on the target and provide maximum kinetic energy to its active missiles on release. Next, the pilot will utilise the Typhoon's high supersonic turn rate to escape from

the threat zone, or to re-attack if necessary. DASS counter-measures and the Typhoon's exceptional agility would be used to deny any enemy the successful use of his weapons.

In Close In Combat, The Typhoon's airframe and engine performance are complemented by its inherent agility. The aircraft has massive subsonic agility, with features such as the Helmet Mounted Sight System (HMSS) enabling heads-out and over-the-shoulder work, exceptional carefree handling, advanced VTAS and DVI technology, and highly effective ASRAAM short range missiles, which are custom-built for close-in and off-boresight lethality. The advanced 'G'-protection system ensures that the pilot remains fully conscious and mobile under the Typhoon's sustained 9G capability.

Mission configuration

Swing-role

The high level of integration and sharing of information between the sub-systems gives the pilot the ability to rapidly assess the overall tactical situation and respond effectively to threats. This capacity for sensor fusion, in combination with a payload that features both air-to-air and air-to-surface weapons, means that the Typhoon is able to switch roles in-flight, making it the most effective swing-role weapon system available.

Air superiority

Today's air defence fighters have to be extremely agile in order to meet the increasingly demanding requirements of subsonic Beyond Visual Range (BVR) combat and supersonic Close In Combat (CIC).

Air interdiction

The Typhoon is capable of delivering a large payload over long distances, day or night, even while retaining a full air-to-air weapons fit. The extensive weapons inventory includes unguided weapons – 'dumb' bombs – and smart munitions which provide increased range, effectiveness and survivability.

Close air support

The Typhoon is ideally suited to the role of close air support, as it can remain on task for long periods of time with large flexible weapon loads. These include extensive air-to-surface weapon configurations systems such as the Paveway IV air-to-ground precision attack weapon as well as retaining full air-to-air capability. Its sophisticated sensor suite allows close co-ordination with ground commanders and the identification of individual targets. Its high

manoeuvrability and sophisticated weaponry allow effective operations over the battlefield.

Weapons

The Typhoon has 13 external stations for weapons and fuel, four on each wing and five on the fuselage with a total payload of over 7,500kg. Its weapon/fuel fit is dependent on requirement and will differ according to the mission configuration – for instance, whether it's performing the close air support role where air-to-ground munitions and additional fuel tanks would dominate, or in the air interdiction role in which case air-to-air munitions would be fitted. The RAF has a large arsenal to draw from including the following:

Litening III Pod

The Litening III (UK) targeting pod, made by Ultra Electronics, is a precision targeting pod that lends the Typhoon a significant edge in combat effectiveness during day, night and under-the-weather conditions in the attack of ground and air targets with a variety of stand-off weapons (laser-guided bombs, conventional bombs and GPS-guided weapons).

BELOW No 11 Squadron Typhoon at Green Flag, USA. The Typhoon is loaded with Enhanced Paveway II bombs, Litening III designator pod and an instrumented tracking pod. *(Geoff Lee/ Eurofighter)*

Developed from an Israeli design by Ultra Electronics working with Rafael, the pod mounts externally and contains a high-resolution, Forward Looking Infra-Red (FLIR) sensor that displays an infra-red image of the target to the pilot. The pod also contains a CCD camera to obtain target imagery in the visible portion of the electromagnetic spectrum.

The pod is equipped with a laser designator for accurate delivery of the Typhoon's laser-guided weapons and a laser rangefinder provides information for the avionics system, such as navigation updates, weapon deliveries and target updates. The Litening pod also includes an automatic target tracker to provide fully automatic, stabilised target tracking at the altitudes, airspeeds and slant ranges consistent with tactical weapon delivery manoeuvres. These features simplify the functions of target detection and recognition, and permit attack of targets with precision-guided weapons on a single pass.

Internal cannon

The Typhoon is equipped with a single Mauser BK-27 cannon that is mounted internally in the fuselage forward of the starboard wing and fires 27mm high-explosive shells. One of the cannon's main strengths is its ability to achieve a full 1,700-rounds-per-minute rate of fire almost from the first round. This is an important asset, particularly if the cannon is being used against a fast-moving target. As with the external weapon loads, targeting of the cannon is through the HUD. When the cannon is selected, a firing predictor is projected onto the HUD, depicting a moving line, or snake, which predicts where the next few rounds of cannon fire will go. The system also incorporates auto-fire, whereby a burst of fire can be automatically engaged when the target passes through the sight.

Air-to-air weapons

ASRAAM

The AIM-132 ASRAAM is a high-speed, highly manoeuvrable, heat-seeking, air-to-air missile, designed as a 'fire-and-forget' weapon that is able to counter intermittent target obscuration in cloud as well as sophisticated infra-red counter measures. Although ASRAAM is predominantly intended for use in the within-visual-range (WVR) arena, it also has capabilities that permit its use in the beyond-visual-range BVR arena.

BELOW No 17 (R) Squadron Typhoon armed with Meteor and ASRAAM missiles. *(BAE Systems)*

AMRAAM

In a typical BVR engagement, the AMRAAM is launched from a range of 20 to 30 nautical miles and is then guided by its own inertial navigation system, while receiving command-guidance updates from the launch aircraft via the data link until it reaches the target area. The missile then enters the final, or terminal phase, where its own monopulse radar detects the target and guides it to impact. The missile is equipped with a radar proximity fuse, which detonates the high-explosive fragmentation warhead at a preset distance from the target. In short-range mode, the missile can be launched 'active-off-the-rail', when the missile's radar detects the target immediately after launch.

Meteor

The Meteor missile is scheduled to enter service with the RAF in 2016. According to its manufacturer MBDA, Meteor has three to six times the kinematic performance of current air-to-air missiles of its type. The key to Meteor's performance is its air-breathing ramjet which boosts the weapon away from the aircraft at over Mach 4 and remains under power until the warhead detonates. This gives the missile the energy to pursue and destroy the fastest and most agile aircraft at range. The warhead carries both impact and proximity fuses so targets can be destroyed even if the missile fails to score a direct hit.

Air-To-Ground Weapons

Brimstone

This advanced radar-guided weapon is derived from the US Army Hellfire AGM-114F missile. Powered by a rocket motor, it can seek and destroy ground-based targets at long range. The weapon locks onto a target after launch and is designed for the attack and destruction of armoured targets. Steerable fins guide the missile with final impact causing a tandem-charge warhead to detonate. The first, smaller warhead nullifies reactive armour, allowing the follow-through charge to penetrate the main armour.

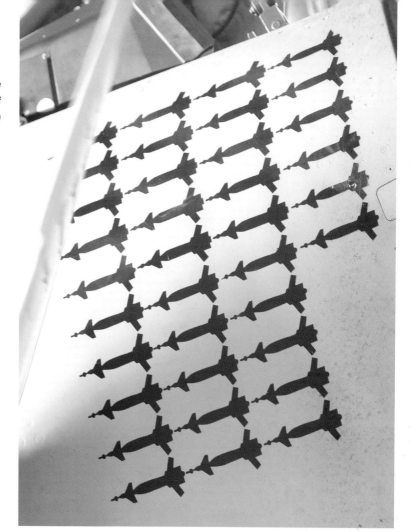
Brimstone has not yet been integrated into the RAF Typhoon's weapons inventory.

Paveway IV

Paveway IV is an advanced, highly accurate precision guided bomb. Equipped with the latest INS and GPS technology and a 500lb warhead, it provides the RAF with an all-weather, 24-hour precision bombing capability able to defeat the majority of general-purpose targets. The weapon is cockpit-programmable and allows the pilot to select weapon impact angle, attack direction and fuzing mode to detonate in airburst, impact or post-impact delay modes. The fuze minimises collateral damage through the ability to detonate the weapon when buried or partially buried, and is fitted with a 'Late-Arm' safety functionality that will not allow an off-course munition to arm. Paveway IV can also be reprogrammed with target data by Forward Air Controllers on the ground.

Storm Shadow

Storm Shadow is arguably the most advanced weapon of its kind in the world. It is equipped with a powerful UK-developed warhead and is designed to attack important hardened targets and infrastructure, such as buried and protected command centres. Mission data, including target details, is loaded into the weapon's main computer before the aircraft leaves on its mission. After release, the wings deploy and the weapon navigates its way to the target at low level using terrain profile matching and an integrated Global Positioning System. On final approach to the target the missile climbs, discards its nose cone and uses an advanced infra-red seeker to match the target area with stored imagery. This process is repeated as the missile dives onto the target, using higher-resolution imagery, to ensure the maximum accuracy. Storm Shadow has not yet been integrated into the RAF Typhoon's weapons inventory.

RIGHT **Loading Paveway II onto a Typhoon at RAF Coningsby.** *(RAF)*

TYPHOON WING STATIONS

Typhoon pilot Flight Lieutenant Nick Graham talks through the aircraft's wing stations, explaining what is hung from which depending on the jet's role:

'On the very extremes of the wing are the DASS Pods – they're the radar jammers, part of the Defensive Aids Sub-System (DASS). Moving in towards the fuselage from those are the ITSPLs – Integrated Tip Stub Pylon Launchers; that's where the ASRAAMs are usually hung. The RAIDs Pods are also hung from that station (Rangeless Airborne Instrumentation Debriefing System housed in the body of a Sidewinder training missile). The next station in from that is the Multi Function Rail Launchers – they can hold either additional ASRAAMs or EPW II (Enhanced

PaveWay) 1,000lb bombs if the aircraft is configured for the ground-attack role.

'The next ones as you move in towards the fuselage are where the 1,000-litre external fuel tanks are hung. Generally, the front line squadrons always fly with two tanks fitted, while 29 (R) Squadron only flies with one tank hung from the centreline station on the fuselage. That's because their sorties are much shorter and have a specific purpose – the student will be practising a specific manoeuvre or module from the OCU syllabus. The only time the aircraft generally fly with three tanks – what's known as a 'ferry fit' – is when they're transiting over long distances such as flying the jets to North America for an

BELOW No 17 (R) Squadron Typhoon FGR4 loaded with Enhanced Paveway II bombs, AMRAAM, ASRAAM, and a centreline drop tank. *(RAF)*

exercise or when they deploy such as on Op Ellamy. It obviously extends the range considerably and reduces the number of times the jets need to meet up with an airborne tanker.

'Moving in, the inboard pylons are generally clean unless the jets are on an active operation such as Ellamy – they would usually then have additional EPW IIs mounted on them. So that's it on the wings – you effectively have four stations on each wing where you can have a mixture of bombs, missiles and fuel tanks.

'On the belly of the aircraft there are additional stations where AMRAAMs can be hung – two on each side, one at the front and one to the rear on each side.'

ABOVE Forward port under-fuselage AMRAAM station. *(Author)*

LEFT The RAIDS (Rangeless Airborne Instrumentation Debriefing System) pod is housed inside the body of a Sidewinder missile occupying the same wing station as the AAM would. *(Author)*

Chapter Five

The pilot's view

'It's a fantastic aircraft to fly from a pilot's perspective – the best. The amount of G you can pull is astonishing – it'll have you at 9G in under a second over a wide operating range. With all that thrust available you can perform some manoeuvres that other jets just aren't capable of.'

Flight Lieutenant Adam Crickmore, pilot, 29 Squadron

OPPOSITE The view from the rear seat of a Typhoon T3 of a XI Squadron Typhoon FGR4 at low level above the British countryside on a routine training sortie. *(RAF)*

Single-seat multi-role fighter jets like the Typhoon are widely considered to be the most complex and demanding aircraft to fly in any air force's fleet. This is primarily due to the workload on the pilot who has to perform two roles, both flying and operating the aircraft, and 'fighting it' – using it as a weapons platform to take out other aircraft, or destroy ground targets.

As jet engines developed and military fighter-bombers became more complex in the aftermath of the Second World War, so the cockpits expanded to accommodate two crew members – the pilot, and a navigator or weapons system operator. This meant that the pilot could concentrate on flying the aircraft from the front seat, while his crewmate focused on managing the radar and delivering the aircraft's weapons effectively.

There are two routes into the Typhoon's cockpit. New pilots – that is, those who have just joined the RAF and have been streamed for fast jet training are still selected in the same way as Harrier pilots were. The rest have made the transition from either the Harrier, or the Tornado F3 (the Harrier was retired from service in December 2010, while the F3 was scrapped in March 2011).

Flight Lieutenant Adam Crickmore

Flight Lieutenant Adam Crickmore joined the Royal Air Force in February 2006 straight from university. He is one of the first 'ab initio' Typhoon pilots – that is, the first person to graduate straight to the Typhoon OCU from flight training. He is 28.

'After completing nine months of officer training at RAF Cranwell, I went straight to elementary flying training on the Tutor T1 at RAF Church Fenton. That takes six months and you graduate with about 60 hours of flying under your belt. I was streamed for fast jets but before you get anywhere near basic fast jet training on the Tucano T1 at RAF Linton-on-Ouse, you visit QinetiQ in Farnborough for centrifuge training. I also spent some time at the RAF Centre of Aviation Medicine at RAF Henlow where I experienced hypoxia in a high-altitude chamber where decompression is induced. It's to give you an idea of what it feels like and how the flying kit we use works.

'Following on from basic fast jet training on the Tucano, you move to RAF Valley in Anglesey. You start off at 208 Squadron, where you spend 28 weeks learning advanced flying training on the Hawk T1, followed by 16 weeks on 19 Squadron where you undertake tactics and weapons training. It's on graduation here that you learn which aircraft you're destined for – either Typhoon or Tornado.

'I was incredibly lucky to be given the Typhoon because there are so few slots available and most of the guys on my course went to the Tornado. From a pilot's perspective, I would have been happy flying anything from a Hercules to a Chinook or a Tornado, but getting the Typhoon felt like winning the lottery! Doing air defence is something I really wanted to do – I wanted to join the Air Force as opposed to the Air *Service* but with the Typhoon being multi-role, I'm getting to do both. To be honest, my expectations have been immeasurably surpassed by the fact that I've ended up flying the Typhoon.

'After RAF Valley, I moved to RAF Coningsby, initially on 29 (R) Squadron, which is the Operational Conversion Unit [OCU] for the

BELOW Flt Lt Adam 'Crickers' Crickmore is one of the RAF's 'ab initio' Typhoon pilots. He graduated straight to the Typhoon OCU on completion of flying training. *(RAF)*

Typhoon. It's here that you learn to fly and fight the aircraft. When you graduate from the OCU, you're posted to one of the front-line Typhoon squadrons. After a short period of training on the squadron, you're finally declared a fully operational combat-ready pilot. It's a long road – it takes roughly five years, and costs an estimated £12.3m to get each Typhoon pilot to this stage.

'You do a lot of simulator work at 29 Squadron. I'd accumulated about ten hours in the sim before my very first trip in a Typhoon. That was in a dual-seat version although the pilot in the back is there simply as a 'safety pilot' so I effectively flew a "ghosted solo". The rest of the syllabus was flown in the simulator with just the odd flight in the jet.

'The Typhoon is a simply astonishing aircraft to fly, an absolute dream. I know everyone talks about the thrust it's got but that's by comparison to the Tornado. For me, coming from the Hawk T1, it's beyond words. There's nothing you can compare it to – the closest analogy I can think of is that it would be like going from a bicycle to a Bugatti Veyron. It has 40,000lbs in reheat, and that amount of thrust is what sets the Typhoon apart from every other fast jet out there.

'I've flown simulated air combat against many other aircraft including the F-15 but the Typhoon just makes everything so easy. Obviously, being fly-by-wire and computer-controlled, the actual hands-on flying couldn't be simpler. The flaps and slats are all automated and you can fly at very low speeds due to the delta wing and the canards at the front. The trim is all controlled by the computer – that's something you do a lot of in flying other aircraft, but on the Typhoon it's completely taken out of the equation. You just set the attitude and you can do whatever you want with the throttles and the aircraft will keep pointing straight where you put it. In any weapons platform, the less work you have to do as a pilot, the less you

have to concentrate on flying. That means you have far more capacity for fighting the aircraft.

'That's basically the ethos behind the Typhoon's whole design. You're not so much a pilot as a systems operator. Obviously, you still have the domestic flying elements such as landing, taking off and refuelling. The flight control systems, the weapons systems and everything else are all focused so that you can spend the maximum amount of time managing the battlespace and performing effectively whatever the mission profile is: air defence, combat air patrols or delivering weapons.

'That said, it's a fantastic aircraft to fly from a pilot's perspective – the best. The amount of G you can pull is astonishing – it'll have you at 9G in under a second over a wide operating range. With all that thrust available, you can perform some manoeuvres that other jets just aren't capable of. If you pull the stick back as hard as you physically can, the Typhoon's computers take that input, perform a few calculations and then turn the aircraft as hard and fast as physics will allow – but without over-stressing the jet.

'Against legacy fighters like the Tornado or the F-15, you may hit a merge [when two fighter aircraft meet head-on, they will usually make a very close, neutral pass, called a "merge"] with another jet and they'll have to use the stick to sort of taper the G so they don't over-stress the jet. In the Typhoon, you just pull the stick back because it's impossible to over-stress it. It will give you up to 9G but you'll never get any more than that in any manoeuvre. As speed starts to taper off, so the G reduces and that's when you can start to taper the pull on the stick to taper the speed. And that, from an operator's perspective, is brilliant because you can spend your time looking at the other aircraft, seeing what it's doing. It means you're doing your best air combat, as opposed to worrying about whether or not you're going to over-stress the jet. So you have the capacity to concentrate on where the other guy is and get weapons on first which is the whole ethos of air combat manoeuvring – there are no prizes for second place!'

Force of nature

An introduction to 'G'

Any technology can only ever be as advanced as the weakest link in the chain. And where aerospace and defence technologies are concerned, the weakest link is human physiology. The only limit to progress is the pilot.

Cutting-edge military jets such as the Typhoon are capable of flying in complete safety under load conditions that are far beyond what the unprotected human body can tolerate, and it's all down to gravity, known by its shorthand, 'G'.

With each change in direction in a violent manoeuvre, the pilot is exposed to acceleration forces corresponding to a multiple of the normal gravitational force on earth (1G). The simplest way to picture how it works is in terms of weight. Weight is a rather abstract concept because the figure we take for granted is weight at ground level. But weight varies according to gravitational force, so if you're exposed to 3G for instance, your weight increases by a multiple of three. That means if you weigh 100kg at ground level, when you experience 3G of force, your weight is 300kg. The current generation of

military jets routinely subject their pilots to 7 to 9 times normal gravitational forces.

G-loads impose different effects on a pilot's physiology according to their nature. Positive acceleration (positive G) is directed upwards, with a downwards reaction that tends to shift the body's organs and blood down while the body's weight increases by the same ratio as the G load. Positive G induces a number of effects on the cardio-circulatory system, including 'pooling', whereby blood flows to the legs and abdominal zone and stagnates there, reducing the flow to the brain and eyes.

This induces hypotension, starving the brain and eyes of sufficient oxygen. This is felt by the pilot first as a so-called 'grey-out' – monochromatic vision (an inability to identify colours) – followed by tunnel vision (limited vision), then 'black-out' (a complete loss of vision). In the most extreme cases this results in G-induced Loss Of Consciousness or G-LOC – also known as 'end point' in that it almost invariably has fatal consequences.

The G-onset, which is the rate of increase in acceleration, plays a central role in the pilot's tolerance towards the effects of G. The more

BELOW This Typhoon is pulling G at max reheat with slats deployed. At this part of the flight envelope it is the foreplanes and the slats that are the primary surfaces for creating lift. *(RAF)*

RIGHT This step-by-step montage shows a pilot in flying suit or 'growbag' (1); in thermal under-suit (2); immersion suit (3). Over the immersion suit, which will protect him from hypothermia in the event of an ejection into the sea during winter months, he wears full-coverage anti-G trousers, anti-G boots and leather flying boots (4), and Typhoon flight jacket (chest counter-pressure garment) and flying gloves (5). With a standard flying helmet and oxygen mask incorporating a microphone, he is ready to fly (6, 7, 8); and finally, wearing a BAE Striker helmet with Helmet-Mounted Display (9).

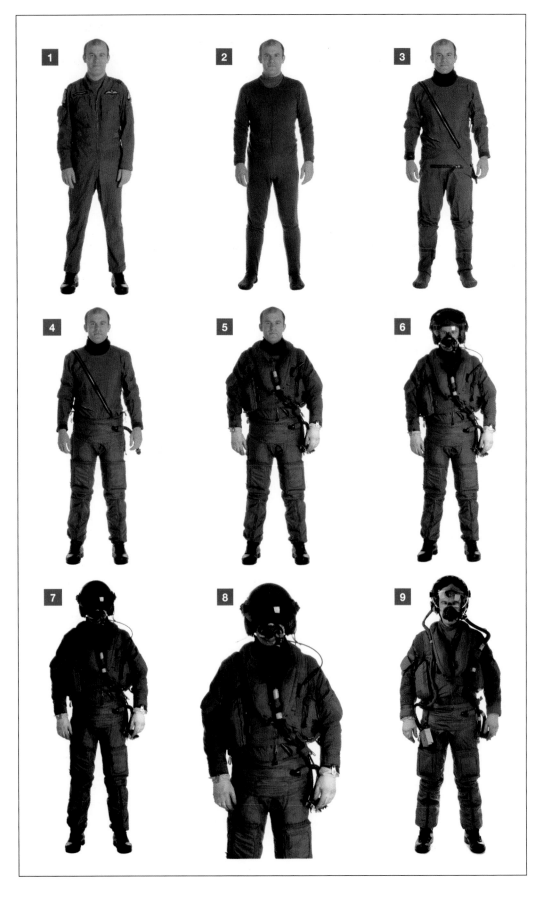

agile the aircraft and the quicker it can generate G forces, the shorter the time between the first experience of impaired vision and total black-out. At G-onset rates of more than 5Gs/sec, which were experienced for the first time in the late 1970s during operational flights in fighters such as the F-16, black-out or even G-LOC can happen instantaneously and without warning.

Negative acceleration (negative G) also increases the body's weight by as many times as the G number, but in the opposite direction. G-multiples become quickly intolerable with an accumulation of blood into the brain leading to the 'red-out' phenomenon followed by the cerebral vessels bursting.

The solution to these problems is the anti-G suit. In simple terms, an anti-G suit comprises special trousers and an abdominal band with air bladders woven into their fabric. When the aircraft (and therefore the pilot) is subjected to a pre-established G load (as measured by an accelerometer), the bladders are automatically inflated by a pneumatic circuit that lets in compressed air. The stretched fabric in the trousers and abdominal band exerts pressure against the lower abdomen, thighs and lower legs that prevents an excessive flow of blood to the lower limbs and facilitates its return to the heart.

The performance potential of modern combat aircraft including the Typhoon cannot be fully exploited, as they expose their pilots to extremely high G-loads. G-onset rates in fourth generation fighters like the Typhoon can be as high as 15–20G/sec, which means the pilot and aircraft reach the maximum permissible acceleration of 10G in less than half a second. The aircraft is of course designed to tolerate this, but the pilot isn't. The physiological threshold is the weakest link in the chain.

Designed as an integral part of the Typhoon's weapon system, the Aircrew Equipment Assembly (AEA) is the most advanced anti-G suit in the world, allowing the pilot to operate the aircraft comfortably and with maximum efficiency. By protecting him from G loads and ensuring safety during ejection, the AEA is designed to enhance survivability on land, at sea or over enemy territory.

The advanced G-protection system ensures that the pilot can operate comfortably in a relaxed G environment under prolonged agile manoeuvring at 9G. The life support system provides pressure breathing and G-protection so that 'pilot-straining' is not necessary under high G-force.

The AEA suit includes full-coverage anti-G trousers combined with a chest counter-pressure garment (CCPG), and adds inflatable bladders to protect the feet. Another vital role of the AEA is to provide thermal and immersion protection to keep the pilot warm and dry even in the coldest and wettest of conditions. Full body protection against NBC threats is also available. To maintain the comfort of the pilot, and therefore retain full operational efficiency, a liquid conditioning system pumps liquid around the upper body to provide heating or cooling as requested. Additional key features of the AEA are inherent fire protection, an integrated automatic life preserver as part of the flight jacket, and the ability to store a number of aircrew survival aids and equipment.

In the event of the possible use of weapons of mass destruction the Typhoon incorporates full NBC filtering systems. In addition the pilot can make use of a newly developed NBC suit, which combined with the flight helmet offers total protection

My first experience of 'G'
Flight Lieutenant Adam Crickmore recounts his first experience of G and how it affected him.

'When you complete elementary flying training, you're sent to QinetiQ at Farnborough to experience G in a centrifuge. Obviously, having only ever done basic flying when I arrived, I had no frame of reference for G so it's hard to know what to expect other than you know you're going to experience a lot of it! The centrifuge at Farnborough consists of an arm with a gondola at one end. It's in a circular room and the arm spins in a circle. The gondola is hinged at the top so it tilts through 90 degrees meaning all the blood is being forced from your head to your feet so the challenge is not to grey out or black out.

'When the centrifuge stops, the gondola returns to right up but your inner ear is obviously still spinning so you feel a tumbling sensation which is really disconcerting. But one thing we learned is just how well the kit works for you. You do the first run without any

G protection at all, so you're dressed in no more than a flying suit [known colloquially as a "grow-bag"]. For your subsequent run, you wear G trousers – the kit that you'll wear when you get to RAF Valley where you fly the Hawk. Once you're in those, you realise that you can pull 6G pretty much without doing anything. It's only when you go higher than 6G that you really need to start tensing the muscles and do anti-G straining manoeuvres.

'I didn't feel sick after my sessions in the centrifuge but what I did feel was the blood pooling in my feet. My calves hurt a lot, and I got the tumbling sensation as well. It all felt pretty strange. I don't think anyone on my course was sick after the centrifuge, but the chaps say it does happen so there are sick bags in the gondola if needed! Some guys blacked out but that was mainly due to poor technique for the anti-G straining manoeuvre.

'Once I'd been selected to fly the Typhoon, I returned to the centrifuge on completion of my advanced flying training on the Hawk T1 at RAF Valley. What was really noticeable then was the difference that the Typhoon kit makes. I was sitting at 9G quite comfortably, and didn't have to do a thing – no anti-G straining manoeuvres, nothing. The Typhoon kit includes a pressure garment in the form of a jacket, which keeps your organs in place so it prevents your heart and lungs from being squeezed out of shape under heavy G. The G trousers cover more of your legs and mid-section, and you also wear anti-G boots and boot innards. They're amazing – they attach to the bottom of the trousers, a bit like a sock, and they inflate as well. With the exception of your arms, you've effectively got all-over anti-G protection. An over-pressure of oxygen is also supplied through the face mask.

'Nobody blacks out using the Typhoon kit – you just relax and the kit does it all for you. Some guys experience a red rash around their mid section after pulling 9G, which I believe is caused by blood vessels breaking in the skin. You can also get what are known as G measles – I get them now and again as tiny little red marks on my forearms after flying but they clear in a day or so.

'G is something that you build up a tolerance to over time but physique plays a huge part in that. Basically, if you had a pilot who was short and squat he'd cope with a lot of G quite easily. On the other hand a tall, slim pilot – someone who ran marathons for instance – would find it particularly hard. It's all down to blood pressure, and the distance between your heart and your head.'

'The sheer amount of thrust the engines deliver is, for me, the most enjoyable and amazing aspect of the whole aircraft. There are few experiences that compare to doing a performance take-off. You engage max reheat and rotate just 8 seconds later. You then accelerate to 250 knots and pull back on the stick to a 60° nose-up attitude, clean her up by bringing the gear up and she'll just keep on climbing. At a guess, I'd say from brakes off to 40,000ft in 90 seconds would be about right. The first time you do it, the guys suggest that you look over your shoulder as you're getting airborne and it's one of the best things about it because you look down and you think, "Amazing! I'm at 25,000ft already and I've only been climbing for a few seconds!" I flew a sortie back here from RAF Valley yesterday – I just put the reheat in and it was literally, "Bye-bye Valley!" It's incredible! There's such an excess of power from the engines that the jet will achieve supersonic speed when climbing in dry power if it's not reined in.

'Speed-wise, we can fly at Mach 2 up at height – the operational ceiling is above 55,000ft and the aircraft is capable of supercruise, so we can maintain supersonic flight without using afterburners. At low level, we're restricted to Mach 1.2 and even then only for a short time – because the air is denser at low level, the airframe heats up. I thought our ceiling was quite high – it's as high as Concorde ever flew and you can see the curvature of the earth from that altitude. But I was chatting to some pilots recently who used to fly the Lightning and one of them took his aircraft up to 82,000ft. He said he got scared because at that point it got a bit dark!

'It's just as impressive in terms of stopping distance as it is in thrust and take-off. The runway at RAF Northolt is quite short at 5,200ft but we can stop in about 3,000ft. That's the sort of distance that would give a C17 a run for its money and that aircraft is famed for its tactical ability to land on very short runways. In the Typhoon we've got low weight allied to

great brakes; it's also got lift dump functionality so when you land, if you push forward on the stick then the canards will drop down to give you extra braking. And of course, it also has a parachute that deploys from the rear to slow you down if you really need it – I can't recall ever having to use it though.

'There's more to the Typhoon than just speed, height and short stopping distances. It can fly slowly as well, although the only time we ever really do that is when we're performing air combat manoeuvres. You never really want to fly slower than 180 knots because it limits your options. There's a built-in system called Auto Low Speed Recovery (ALSR) which stops the aircraft departing from controlled flight at high angles of attack. It's part of the Flight Control System so it's able to detect a developing low-speed situation. If it does, you get an audible and visual warning. It's basically the aircraft saying, "Right you, ease off on the pull, or increase the throttles otherwise in a minute, I'm gonna take it off you!" If you're unable to react or you ignore the warning, the ALSR will actively take control of the aircraft, select maximum dry power for the engines and return the jet to a safe flight condition depending on the attitude by either using an ALSR "push"', "pull" or "knife-over" manoeuvre. At that point, you have control again.

'In addition to Auto Low Speed Recovery, the Typhoon also has a Disorientation Recovery

system that you can bring into play via a button on the console just forwards and to the right of the stick. You can't miss it – it's surrounded by a yellow base with diagonal black stripes across it. So let's imagine you're flying in cloud and you suffer a bad case of the leans. You're looking at all your references but you still can't work out which way is up so you hit that button and the aircraft will simply roll level with the horizon with a slight nose-up attitude.

'The cockpit in the Typhoon has to be one of the best places in any aircraft for a pilot to sit. The ergonomics are absolutely top-notch so it's a very clean, comfortable and uncluttered environment with all the information a pilot could wish for. You sit relatively high which means that, as well as having great visibility to the front, sides and back via the bubble canopy, you also get very good visibility down both sides too.

'One of the breaks from the norm in this aircraft is that the HUD is the main source of flight information and reference. It has a much larger display area than on other fast jets and all relevant data is clearly and readily accessible without you having to look down. With the new helmets, you also get it through a projection onto the visor. If the HUD were to fail for any reason, you have the option to replicate its information on one of the screens so you've got plenty of options. What it means is that the three display screens are given over to more

ABOVE **Pulling G at high altitude, with slats deployed to generate lift and foreplanes maintaining stability, while flying air combat manoeuvres in a 3 (F) Squadron Typhoon.** *(RAF)*

RAF TYPHOON MANUAL

relevant head-down information – weapons fit, engine instruments, moving map display, etc. They're also infinitely configurable, so you can swap information from one screen to another if you want to, although we tend to keep it to a standard configuration. There's a cursor that you can move across the screens to control the information on them and make selections. It's located on the throttle body – you use the fourth and middle fingers to control it.

'You can call up the weapons fit at any given time on the screens – when you select it, you get a birds-eye view of the jet showing each station and its ordnance along with your chaff, flares, rounds remaining and your fuel tanks. We carry a different weapons fit depending upon our tasking, so for an air-to-air sortie, we take six AMRAAMs and two ASRAAMs. AMRAAMS are mounted close to the body and the ASRAAMS are on the wing pylons. We also usually fly with two wing tanks to extend our range and patrol time.

'You select the weapons using the stick. There's a trigger on the front operated by your index figure – that's for the air-to-air missiles, or guns for ground attack. The weapon selector is operated by a top hat controlled by your thumb – so forwards and you've got your AMRAAMS, press it down you've got your ASRAAMS, and then bring it back for the gun.

'The fit was completely different when we were based at RAF Northolt to protect London during the Olympic Games in 2012. The aircraft were in a completely clean configuration with no wing tanks because the priority, once we'd launched and dealt with whatever threat presented, was to get back on the ground as quickly as possible. If we'd been carrying extra fuel in wing tanks, we'd have had to spend time burning it off to get us down to landing weight. The clean configuration obviously made a massive difference to how quick the aircraft felt – the thrust available taking off on full combat reheat with no wing tanks was immense, just beyond words. An already quick aircraft suddenly became even quicker.

'An average month for us on squadron sees us on QRA [Quick Reaction Alert – often abbreviated to "Q"] roughly three times in 28 days – a Q shift runs to 24 hours at a time. Our squadron has been pretty busy recently what

with us covering London during the Olympics, and some of our pilots down in the Falklands. On top of all that, we fly training sorties to stay current and practise manoeuvres. Yesterday for example, I was airborne at 15:00 for a short hop to Wales to fly some low-level sorties. We fly cycles – takeoffs and landings, touch-and-goes out of Coningsby a few days each month – it's basically all about us staying at the top of our game. I average about 20 hours flying a month.

'We've also got secondary duties on top of the flying so every day is different but, usually, I'm at work by 08:30hrs. If I'm going to be flying in the first wave of the day, we'd have our briefing and aim to be airborne for 10:30hrs. Depending on the profile of the sortie, we'll be flying for up to two hours. One day we might practice air combat manoeuvres, flying head-to-head against other pilots in the squadron. On another, we might mount a combat air patrol so we'd need to refuel air-to-air from a tanker.

'Once we're back on the deck we'll debrief so we'll conclude somewhere around 14:00hrs. Grab some food and we'll probably spend the afternoon on secondary duties, admin – stuff like that. Alternatively, we could be into another flight so there'll be another brief and then the flying cycle begins again.'

Squadron Leader Ryan Mannering

Squadron Leader Ryan Mannering was an experienced Tornado pilot with 14 Squadron when he was posted in 2007 to the Typhoon OCU. On completion of the course, he was appointed the Officer Commanding Typhoon Training Flight at RAF Coningsby.

'Back in the summer of 2007 I was a pilot with 14 Squadron enjoying my third tour on the Tornado GR4 at Exercise Anatolian Eagle in Turkey. On the second Monday of the detachment I was called into the office for a chat with the boss: I was told to return to base which, at that time, was RAF Lossiemouth. My heart sank and I began to wonder what I'd done! As it happened, it was good news – I was posted to 29(R) Squadron to undertake the Typhoon OCU.

'I was thrilled and somewhat smug at the number of "green-eyed monsters" that

OPPOSITE **No 11 Squadron Typhoon F2 max reheat take-off.** *(RAF)*

appeared when the decision was announced to the rest of the squadron. But before attending the OCU I had to go through extensive pre-employment training. This started with a trip to the Centre of Aviation Medicine at RAF Henlow to understand the physiological effects of flying such a high-performance aircraft and to get to grips with pressure breathing now that I would be able to attain altitudes in excess of 55,000ft in my new steed. I was also subjected to rapid decompression at 45,000ft in a hypobaric chamber.

'I was kitted out with my new Aircrew Equipment Assemblies (AEA) including a new G-suit – full coverage anti-G trousers and pressure jerkin. The next trip was to Farnborough to undergo centrifuge training, experiencing up to 9G and passing the mandatory high-G qualification run that saw me fit to proceed with the training. With my centrifuge experience fresh in my mind I was subject to two high-G sorties in the Centre of Aviation Medicine Hawk aircraft based at Boscombe Down. This is performed in full Typhoon AEA and is designed to give you confidence in the kit. I was pleasantly surprised to find that I could comfortably maintain 6G without any kind of straining and flying at 9G was easily achievable. My final port of call was to the National Air Traffic Control Centre at Swanwick in Hampshire. The Typhoon generates

BELOW Pairs. *(RAF)*

so much thrust that it can out-climb radar updates so I got a first-hand demonstration of the pitfalls and advantages of the jet's exceptional rate of climb and service ceiling!

'Despite being so eager to get my hands on the aircraft, I was forced to wait a little longer as there was a four-week ground school phase to attend at the Typhoon Training Facility [TTF] at RAF Coningsby, the MOB HQ of the Typhoon Force. The Ground School phase consisted of two weeks of classroom technical instruction where the complexity of the aircraft and the various fleets of Typhoon became all too apparent. There was a graduated migration to the Typhoon simulators to undertake basic conversion and emergency procedure training. TTF utilises Aircrew Synthetic Training Aids (ASTA) a four-nation project consisting of two Full Mission Simulators (FMS) and two Cockpit Trainers (CTs). The four-week phase culminates in a simulator check ride consisting of an instrument flying training sortie with full emergency procedure training and examinations on Typhoon technical data and emergency procedures.

'At last it was time to start the conversion phase. My first sortie consisted of general handling followed by instrument flying and circuit practice, but all I can really remember is grinning at the acceleration of the aircraft that was only in dry power but had the ability to climb at 20° nose-up at 400 knots. The other lasting impression is of a very clean uncluttered cockpit with three Multi-Function Head Down Displays and wide-angle HUD with all the information a pilot could wish for!

'The conversion phase consists of five sorties including an IRT then first solo, followed by a formation ride and a night check ride. The first solo, usually in a single-seat aircraft as opposed to a "tub" (twin-seat Typhoon), usually involves the pilot enjoying the awesome performance of the aircraft at low level, either in the Lake District or Wales, followed by a transit at FL500 or above just because you can. Such is the performance of the aircraft at low level that it is imperative to use the auto-throttle set to 420 knots to avoid encroaching the transonic region, creating a sonic boom and causing untold complaints!

'With the conversion phase complete, it was time to start the tactical portion of the

syllabus. The Typhoon Force Basic Counter Air Module (BCAM) OCU syllabus aims to teach the pilot basic Air Defence (AD) skills. The aim is for the pilot to be able to fight the aircraft firstly Within Visual Range (WVR) employing the ASRAAM, then work up to Beyond Visual Range (BVR) utilising the AMRAAM, and then finally combining all the disciplines as a tactical pair. The WVR phase involved two synthetic events and seven live-flying events covering offensive, defensive and high-aspect fighter manoeuvring. This phase was highly demanding physically owing to the high G-loading on your body and the manipulation of the weapon system. Typhoon human-to-machine interface is ergonomically superior to many aircraft in service, utilising Voice Throttle And Stick (VTAS) inputs to control the weapon system; it's very much a home-away-from-home for the play-station generation.

'The BVR phase consisted of three synthetic events and four live-flying events working up from one-versus-one intercepts to one-versus-two at low level employing AMRAAM then ASRAAM tactics. It was during this phase that I started to become aware of the vast amount of information the aircraft had to offer, and the consequent temptation to stay "heads-in", soaking it all up.

'The BVR phase moved swiftly on to the Pairs phase. This consisted of three synthetic events and six flying events culminating in a pair of Typhoons, with me as the wingman, fighting an unknown pair of hostile aircraft in a variety of different presentations. The pairs element of the OCU was undeniably the most tactical and most demanding with the introduction of defensive aids and data link (MIDS/Link16) manipulation.

'The final part of the course is the Quick Reaction Alert phase which enables a graduate from 29 (R) Squadron to be declared Limited Combat Ready and thus able to undertake the 24/7, ten-minute notice-to-launch for NATO and UK duties.

'Upon graduation, pilots are posted to one of the frontline Typhoon squadrons. Here the young graduate will go on to complete an Advanced Counter Air Module (ACAM), and for selected individuals, the Basic and Advanced Surface to Air Module (BSAM/ASAM).'

ABOVE A 29 (R) Squadron twin-seat Typhoon T3 at 90 degrees to the horizon as it flies at low level through a valley in Wales. Low flying is a perishable skill so regular sorties are essential. At 250ft above sea level and 7 miles a minute, there's no room for error. *(Lloyd Horgan)*

Once ground crew have prepped the aircraft (1) and (4), the aircraft are 'armed' and ready (2). Once prepped, they wait on the flight line (3). Flt Lt Adam Crickmore takes his seat on the flight line; (5) strapping in and pre-flight checks (7-10). *(RAF, except for 1 and 3, Nick Robinson)*

Pre-flight checks done, it's mask on (11) and signal to ground crew for engine start (12); close the canopy (13); engage flight resident software (14); clear the groundcrew away from the aircraft prior to taxying (15); the Typhoon taxies (16); once clearance is received for take-off, the engines are cycled up to full reheat and the brakes released for a performance take-off (17). *(RAF, except for 14 Nick Robinson)*

The Typhoon rockets down the runway (18) and just 8 seconds later leaves the ground having covered just 2,000ft. The pilot selects 'gear up' (19) and pulls back on the stick (20). As the aircraft storms skywards, it's not actually flying; rather, it's become a rocket and is propelled to altitude on a cushion of its own power (21). *(RAF)*

BASIC FIGHTER MANOEUVRES

Basic Fighter Manoeuvres (BFM) are tactical movements that a fighter pilot makes during air combat manoeuvring or dogfighting in order to gain a positional advantage over an opponent. Achieving this will allow him to get 'guns on' and fire first.

BFM consist of tactical turns, rolls, and other actions to get behind or above an enemy, before the opponent can do the same. They can be offensive, to help a pilot get behind an enemy, or defensive, to help him evade an attacker's weapons. BFM can also be neutral – this occurs where both opponents strive for an offensive position, or disengagement manoeuvres, to help facilitate an escape.

Air combat forms part of the fundamental training that all RAF fighter pilots receive, and begins on the Tucano at RAF Linton-on-Ouse. It's a level playing field in so far as the pilots are flying the same aircraft and pit their skills against each other. Things step up a level when they move to RAF Valley to fly the Hawk and reach their peak at the OCU. As qualified front-line pilots, they regularly fly exercises against pilots from other NATO forces in different aircraft, which more resembles real aerial combat and means they must learn to cope with different technological advantages and weapons.

Air combat takes place in a three-dimensional arena so BFM aren't limited by simple two-dimensional turns, as displayed during a car chase. BFM rely on each pilot's ability to make trade-offs between airspeed (kinetic energy) and altitude (potential energy) as much as an aircraft's turn performance. This is in order to maintain an energy level that will allow the fighter to continue manoeuvring efficiently. Fighter pilots need a comprehensive understanding of the geometry of pursuit within the three-dimensional arena, where different angles of approach result in different rates of closure. The fighter pilot uses these angles not only to get within a range where weapons can be used, but also to avoid flying out in front of the opponent or crossing his flight path.

The most advantageous position is usually above or behind the opponent – the aircraft or pilot occupying this space is the attacker. Conversely, the defending pilot is usually either below or ahead of the opponent.

Most BFM are offensive. Defensive manoeuvres more often consist of turning very aggressively to avoid the attacker's weapons – either tightening, relaxing or reversing the turn. The defending pilot will usually attempt to force an overshoot, or to extend the range sufficiently for him to dive away and escape.

Flight Lieutenant Nick Graham

Nick is an instructor with the Typhoon OCU on 29 (R) Squadron at RAF Coningsby. He was previously a Tornado F3 pilot before transferring to the Typhoon in 2008.

'I was lucky enough to get a ten-month bursary from the RAF while I was at Salford University so I did my Elementary Flying Training at the University Air Squadron there prior to graduating in 1997 to join the RAF. I was streamed for fast jets and arrived at RAF Coningsby in 2001 on the Tornado F3 OCU. Following successful completion of the course, I was posted to RAF Leuchars for four years, initially on 43 Squadron and latterly 111 Squadron. Then I was selected for an exchange tour and went to Denmark where I flew the F-16 for three years.

'That was fascinating and a real privilege. The F-16 was a massive step up from the F3, avionically advanced and superior to what I'd been used to but, for all that, it was a very simple aeroplane to fly. The F3 was all bells and whistles, moving of levers and big crank handles. It had about 14 or 15 different items on the pre-landing checklist alone and you'd struggle to get them all in from the start of the downwind leg to the start of the final turn. In the F-16, it was "Speed below 250 knots, gear down" and that was it! It's pretty similar to the

ABOVE Nick Graham flew from RAF Coningsby in the practice diamond-nine formation by RAF Typhoons for the Royal Jubilee celebrations. This is the formation over Lincolnshire the day before the aircraft were due to fly over Windsor Castle as part of the RAF's contribution to events. (RAF)

OPPOSITE Single-seater. A Royal Air Force Typhoon pilot enters the cockpit as the sun sets over Gioia del Colle, southern Italy. (RAF)

Typhoon in that regard. The F-16 is multi-role too – air-to-air or air-to-ground. I learned a lot on that exchange which has proved useful later in my career. It taught me how to use a targeting pod and smart weapons, which gave me something of a head start when I was posted to the Typhoon OCU.

'You run out of superlatives where the Typhoon's performance is concerned but the amount of G you can pull in it is astonishing. You literally don't have to do anything at all until about 6 or 7G – and even then you only have to put a bit of effort in to stop yourself seeing stars or experiencing a shortage of blood to the head. It's not like pulling 6G in any other aircraft – the kit we wear is really, really brilliant. It allows you to persist, to gain the advantage over everyone else – it gives you pressure breathing and all sorts of other stuff to keep you one step ahead. It means that when we're on exercise and we go and fight the F-15s (which we inevitably win!) you finish the fight and you're ready for the next one. You call them over the radio and ask them to tell you when they're ready for the next fight and you can hear it in their voices when they reply – that guy's been

working really hard, he's out of breath when he's talking to you. It means we can go and do the fight again and again and feel as fresh as a daisy. And it means that over time, as a corps of pilots, you can keep doing that job for a long, long time. It's just another edge that Typhoon gives you.

'I did the Jubilee fly-past in 2012 as an airborne spare. If anything had gone wrong with one of the other aircraft before going in, they'd have peeled off and I'd have slotted in. The fly-past was on the Saturday so we flew a practice run on the Friday – a bit of practice, a bit of filming and then I came back to Coningsby while they went on a round robin across Lincolnshire. On the Saturday we launched as an 11-ship for the run down to Windsor – it was like one of those World War II posters with all these contrails drawn across the morning sky. We flew to the south coast and let down to low level, and just hung around until we got to our timing point over the Isle of Wight, and then they pressed in while I peeled off.

'I needed to be up at 40,000ft for the transit back so I talked to civilian air traffic control and they gave me clearance to climb. I had loads of

fuel so I accelerated to 500 knots, put the jet on its backside and went to 40,000ft. As I was in the climb, air traffic control came on the radio and said, "Report on passing 10,00ft" and I was like, "Er... passing 20,000, 30,000, at 40,000ft" They asked me what my heading was – "Er, don't have one!"

'Often now they'll say "no restrictions" when they're talking to us about climbs or descents. We can descend incredibly quickly over a point in the ground. You scrub off all your speed, then point the nose at the ground and almost do a spin and the jet does a velocity vector roll – you often see them at air shows – where it kind of spins around a given point in space, but at the ground. You ideally want to stay as high as you can for as long as you can because it burns next to no fuel. From an air traffic control perspective, they're getting really antsy because you're coming up against what is effectively a wall in the sky and they think you're going to go though it into controlled airspace. But you know that you can virtually throw the aircraft at the ground and get to low level with almost no forward movement and simply nip out at the bottom. They'll be on the radio going, "Just confirm you're going to descend?" and you're like, "Yeah, yeah... watch this!" It's because we're moving faster than their radar can report so the information they're seeing on the screen is already out of date as it appears.

'There's something really cool for me about walking out to an aeroplane with just one seat in it. You get a bit of a rush when you walk up to it. You think, "Wow, there's no room for anyone else. That is literally your own little aeroplane." And with this jet particularly, you think, "I want to be up there," and you can just do it. With a heavy left hand, you move the stick and bam! – you're right where you want to be almost as quick as you can think it. It's amazing. It really is a very, very cool aircraft.

'For me though, the best aspect of this job is on a really crappy day where the cloud cover is endless and renders daylight into dark. Grey, steely skies, miserable days. In winter, I can get particularly miserable if I don't see the sun so I have to pinch myself sometimes that I can just strap into a jet and punch through the clag into a world of bright, warm sunshine and endless blue skies. It really doesn't get any better than that.'

Chapter Six

The Engineer's view

'The individual components on Typhoon are a lot more serviceable and robust than they were on the Tornado or Harrier. The engine is a prime example – it's truly state-of-the-art and you just don't get the same sort of failures that dogged the RB199 and the Pegasus.'
Squadron Leader Mark Butterworth, SENGO, 11 Squadron

OPPOSITE **An XI Squadron technician runs a diagnostics check on a Typhoon in a HAS at RAF Coningsby. Above him, on the fuselage front section, the avionics bay doors are open.** *(Author)*

All first-line engineering and maintenance on the RAF aircraft is handled at squadron level, headed up by a Squadron Leader known as 'SENGO' – the Senior ENGineering Officer. Reporting to him are two JENGOs – Junior ENGineering Officers holding the rank of Flight Lieutenant – each heading up one shift of technicians. The Typhoon needs just three engineering trades to keep it maintained – Mechanics, Avionics and Weapons.

The most junior rank in RAF engineering is held by Aircraft Maintenance Mechanics (AMMs). AMMs are Avionics and Mechanical technicians in the making and the rank represents the entry level for the RAF's aircraft technicians. AMMs are responsible for the day-to-day handling, flight servicing and general husbandry of the aircraft. AMMs carry out routine tasks on the Typhoon such as tyre inflation, refuelling, engine oil replenishment and canopy cleaning.

After roughly 18 months, AMMs return to RAF Cosford for further technical training. Successful graduates then become Avionics or Mechanical Technicians and are posted to one of the Typhoon squadrons based at RAF Leuchars and RAF Coningsby.

Squadron Leader Mark Butterworth

Squadron Leader Mark Butterworth is 11 Squadron's SENGO or Senior Engineering Officer.

'As SENGO, I'm responsible for all the engineering effort that takes place by all personnel on the squadron in order to generate and maintain the aircraft. I look to maximise the availability, capability and air worthiness of all the aircraft allocated to 11 Squadron.

'On a day-to-day basis, we have individual shifts of engineers to carry out the flight servicing activities on the aircraft that are flying, and to carry out maintenance on any aircraft that are unserviceable for any reason. That's all looked after by JENGO, the flight lieutenants responsible for each shift. Among my responsibilities is being on hand to offer advice on any particularly difficult issues they have.

'On each shift we have specialists in three trades who, between them, look after every aspect of engineering on the Typhoon. Mechanical technicians are responsible for the airframes and the engines so that encompasses the hydraulics, the fuel, the structure and the surface of the aircraft itself, everything to do with the engines and the secondary power systems. Avionics technicians are responsible for the cockpit instruments, monitoring and maintaining the data buses, the avionics suite – anything electrical or avionics-related, or pretty much anything to do with the cockpit. Weapons technicians look after all of the weapons that

BELOW **Squadron Leader Mark Butterworth.** *(RAF)*

we fit to the aircraft as you might expect but they're also responsible for any other role-specific equipment we might fit such as external fuel tanks, targeting pods, reconnaissance or training pods – if it fits on the ASRAAM rails or it's ordnance, it falls under their remit.

'They also look after the ejector seat for the simple reason that it's armed – it needs rocket motors to get it and the pilot out of the aircraft safely so they make sure the explosive components are all within life and fit for purpose. The Typhoon was designed as a three-trade aircraft – it's just one area where simplicity comes into play and makes everyone's life easier. The safety equipment trade also falls under my umbrella – it's responsible for the pilots' flying gear, including the flares within their jackets.

'There are a lot of grey areas so none of the trades are exclusive. If you take something like the armament control system which is a series of data buses and black boxes that talk to one another, it's not the exclusive remit of the avionics technicians – the weapons guys will also be involved, so the two trades will be working together to solve the problem. I guess that's another area where Typhoon differs from say Harrier or Tornado – the armourers aren't just responsible for hanging equipment from the wings and the fuselage as they might be on other frames. Here they have to be technologically minded because they have to deal with avionics issues that impact on their systems. Very few problems fit neatly into a little box saying "mechanical snag" or "avionics snag" – the nature of the Typhoon means that the trades have to work together.

'To me, that's a real strength because it develops our tradesmen and gives them a much bigger and deeper understanding of where their systems sit on the aircraft in terms of the big picture. There's a lot of cross-fertilisation of ideas and skills.

'We don't drill down too deeply when it comes to engineering on the Typhoon – in terms of mechanics, there really isn't a lot we can do compared with something like the Tornado F3 which was all analogue – linkages, levers, dials, etc. Typhoon is the polar opposite of that, a digital aircraft that's almost all "plug-and-play". We deal in line-replaceable items

so, for example, we'd replace a brake unit, but we wouldn't deal with something like replacing the brake disc within that unit. Really in-depth maintenance is handled by the second-line engineering team at RAF Coningsby, which is a separate division with BAE engineers and technicians on staff.

'We have to be fairly all-encompassing in terms of first-line engineering at squadron level because we are an expeditionary force – we don't have the luxury on deployment of being able to call on a second-line unit so we have to have the capability of being able to deal

BELOW Weapons engineers work on the Mk 16A ejector seat. *(Author)*

ABOVE Avionics bay maintenance. (Nick Robinson)

with pretty much whatever is thrown up at us while away. We won't break components down to their constituent parts – we'll just change the components themselves. Here on station we have specialist bays for a lot of the major components – there's a wheel bay, an engine bay, an avionics bay looking after all the different avionics suites on the aircraft. There's a gun bay for the armourers and a seat bay to handle any maintenance on the Martin Baker Mk16a ejector seat.

'We fix aircraft when they're broken so, for instance, if there's a fuel or hydraulic leak, we'll replace the pipes that contain the fluids in order to deal with the leak. But the majority of what we have to deal with at squadron level can be solved similarly to problems with a PC at home – a sort of Ctrl-Alt-Delete reboot of the system. That probably solves 90% of the problems that might flash up on the cockpit screens. The 10% that fall outside of that are usually sorted by replacing one black box with another. To identify where the fault is, we plug the aircraft into a diagnostic unit in much the same way as car mechanics – who are more like technicians now – when the engine management light comes on in your car. It tells us what the fault is and what component we need to replace.

'The only time we ever really get any problems outside of that is wiring faults where we have to replace the wire. As you might imagine, it can be a nightmare task because of the sheer amount of wiring on the Typhoon, especially if you have to chase down a single failure in a wire which could be 15 metres long. It gets really complicated if we have to strip down a bay to get to a specific 15 metre wire, remove it, replace it and join it into the existing circuits, then rebuild the bay – that sort of activity can take a week to carry out and that means an airframe out of action for the duration. That's about as complicated as it gets at squadron level.

'We try to run maintenance opportunities in parallel so if we have an aircraft that we know has a wiring snag and it's going to be out of action for a week then we'll try and take the opportunity to conduct as many other maintenance activities on it as possible.

'The individual components on Typhoon are a lot more serviceable and robust than they were on either the Tornado or Harrier – and I've worked on all three so I have a pretty good idea! The Typhoon's in a different league really, it's so far advanced it's difficult to even draw a comparison. The engine is a prime example – it's truly state-of-the-art and you

RIGHT **EJ200 maintenance at Coningsby.**
(Geoff Lee/Eurofighter)

just don't get the same sort of failures that dogged both the Harrier's Pegasus engine and the RB199 in the F3. Gearboxes were a problem on those, as was the number of individual components that failed such as the fuel feed. The EJ200 is more than a generation on from those – the Harrier and Tornado are third-generation fighters whereas the Typhoon is 4.5 so it's streets ahead.

'A lot of the simple mechanical problems that you would have had on basic components on those third-gen engines you just don't get with this one because it's been so incredibly well designed. Also, the support we get from Rolls-Royce and the preventative maintenance that we carry out goes a long way to ensuring that we pick up any potential faults before they ever have a chance to develop. We'll use a boroscope on the engine – basically putting a small camera inside it so we can examine the surfaces to ensure there are no cracks, fatigue or other damage. The RB199 and Pegasus engines were both susceptible to FOD [Foreign Object Damage] on the surface of the blades which would then propagate down through the engine but you just never see that sort of damage to the EJ200 – certainly not to anything approaching the same degree. That's partly a result of how high the engine intakes are sited but also down to the manufacturing process used on the blades – the tolerances are far, far better.

'That really came through on Operation Ellamy, in Libya, where we only changed one engine the whole period we were out there – and it later transpired that this had been unnecessary. Contrast that with the GR4s on Ellamy – they were changing engines on a weekly basis, largely as a result of FOD. The EJ200 is just so much more resilient. In fact, resilience is almost like a theme that runs like a thread through the whole aircraft. Take the inertial navigation units that we had on the Harriers – you'd put one in and it would sometimes take three or four flights before you could tell if it was going to be stable. If it wasn't, you'd have to change it and the whole cycle

would start again. On Typhoon, the avionics suite has been designed to diagnose its own faults so the aircraft is telling you what the problems are rather than you having to go and hunt them down.

'The radar is another example of how simple life has become for us. On the Tornado, the radar had so many LRIs [Line-Replaceable Items – the components that constitute the radar] that diagnosing whatever module had a fault in was like searching for a needle in a haystack. We used to joke that you'd be better off rolling a dice and changing whatever numbered module the dice came up with. You could spend weeks chasing a radar snag on the F3 and when you found a set of LRIs that worked, you'd want to seal them and never touch them again!

'On Typhoon, it's so much more straightforward. It's more powerful, but of a far simpler design from our perspective so it takes fewer modules to do the job. The aircraft effectively gives us clues as to which line-replaceable item needs replacing so again, we're not spending half our time trying to diagnose a fault before we can identify a solution. If you change a component or module,

the radar carries on working as well as it ever did – there's no trying to cajole it, it won't throw other modules out of synch. You replace whichever one is faulty and the whole thing works again. That alone massively reduces the downtime because you don't have to wait a few weeks after major maintenance to see how it goes. There's no crossing of fingers, no alchemy – everything works exactly as it should. It really is plug-and-play – you take one component out, plug another in its place and away you go.

'That said, you still have to know and understand the technology that underpins everything – the theory, how it all fits together, the principles behind the radar, fuel system and engine. Because as much as it's potentially a case of "black box out, black box in", you still need to be able to troubleshoot – what could cause x or y fault to arise? We still need our technicians to be as skilled as they ever were – it's just that they have a different skill set now.

'One of the things I really like is that we have a real mixture of guys who are new to the RAF and have only ever worked on Typhoon, and guys who have come from the Harrier and Tornado fleet – even the helicopter fleet. So they come in with fault-finding skills and we're able to blend all those skills together which makes the guys, as individuals, far better technicians than they were before.

'There aren't any weaknesses from an engineering perspective on the Typhoon like there were on Tornado or Harrier. The F3's radar was a great piece of kit in terms of its effectiveness but it was difficult to get working. On the Harrier, you always wanted to get the engine to output the right amount of power to allow it to hover but it took a long time and a lot of finesse to get it to do that, which I always thought kind of ironic given that was its party piece. The Typhoon just doesn't have an Achilles' heel like that.

'Things tend to go in cycles. We might have a couple of weeks where we have power-up problems but then they'll disappear and we'll go a period where nothing seems to go wrong. Generally, because the aircraft is so good at monitoring its own performance it tends to tell us in advance so problems never really get a chance to develop.

'Bird strikes aren't something we tend to see much evidence of on Typhoon. If they go down the air intakes, there's a very good chance we'll never know a thing about it because once they get to the engine, they're effectively vaporised. One or two small birds versus the blades and heat of an EJ200 jet engine – it's not exactly a fair fight! Often the only way you know is because you can smell the blood on the air intake or see a few streaks of blood actually in the intake cowling. On the other hand, if it swallows it clean and it goes down the intake without touching the sides, we'll never know it happened.

'It's an amazing aircraft from an engineering perspective really – it likes flying fast, so we don't have any problems with it when it flies fast. It likes flying long sorties – we don't get any problems when it flies long sorties. It likes being out in hot, sunny weather – so we don't get any problems when it's based in hot, sunny climates. That said, nothing – whether it's a watch, a car or an aeroplane – likes being out in direct sun for an extended period of time so we take precautions by putting the aircraft under a sun shelter.

'The Tornado GR4 force currently has five

squadrons in Afghanistan, so they're able to rotate through with a degree of room to breathe. The Typhoon force only has four operational squadrons from which they have to provide pilots and aircraft for QRA [Quick Reaction Alert] at RAF Leuchars and RAF Coningsby, then there's the Falkland Islands QRA which we have to provide pilots and engineers for. The Harrier Force supported Afghanistan with just three squadrons but the constant rotation of aircraft and personnel meant they were simply spread too thin – and they didn't have any other operational commitments like QRA to provide for. There's no reason why Typhoon couldn't support Operation Herrick.

'There are also strategic aspects to my role. For instance, I took the lead in planning our deployment to RAF Northolt for London 2012. That had some unique elements to it. For instance, we were moving to a site that hadn't existed previously – we were taking over one half of a taxiway at RAF Northolt which had to be expanded for us. They also put up rapid-erect shelters to house the aircraft and portable cabins for us to operate from. I spent a lot of time putting together an IT network in terms of what we needed by way of comms – both

Inspecting the APU exhaust. *(Nick Robinson)*

Gearbox oil change. *(Nick Robinson)*

Checking the Air Data Transducers (ADT). *(Nick Robinson)*

Refuelling team and vehicle. *(Nick Robinson)*

Refueller at work. *(Nick Robinson)*

phones and computers – and other equipment. I had to liaise with the explosives licensing people to advise them of our needs so that they understood what we had to do but working within the constraints of what they were happy with in terms of safe distances. I established links with the local engineers at Northolt – both service and civilian so we knew ahead of time where we'd be able to get support from while we were there. We were using live weapons so we had to make sure our guys were aware of any differences in respect of how we do things at Coningsby and how they do them at Northolt. Bear in mind that at Coningsby we have a permanent, long-established base whereas at Northolt we were operating out of a temporary base set up just for the duration of the Olympics.

'Our being there meant we had to impose restrictions on a lot of Northolt's other users given that we were using fast jets armed with live weapons and most of the traffic in and out consists of private jets, conventional RAF aircraft and helicopters. However awkward things might have been for us as the visitors, they would have been far more difficult for the base's resident squadrons and personnel. As seamless as shifting our Southern QRA cover to RAF Northolt was, I can't imagine any of the base's permanent residents were too upset to see us leave!'

Flying Officer Stephanie Wilde

Flying Officer Stephanie Wilde is one of the two JENGOs at XI Squadron, her first posting after completion of training.

"I started Initial Officer Training (IOT) in February 2008 and was awarded my Comission in October that year. Following IOT, I commenced my phase two engineering specific training at the Defence College of Aeronautical Engineering at RAF Cranwell, a 30-week course which built on my engineering degree and including academic modules, engineering management and a two-week exercise which simulates working on a flying Squadron. During Engineer Officer Foundation Training (EOFT) I was told I had been posted to XI Squadron as one of

two Junior Engineering Officers (JENGO). Since completing my training, it has been a very quick process – I graduated from EOFT on the Friday, arrived at RAF Coningsby the following Monday and flew to Turkey on detachment on the Wednesday. My first three weeks on the job were spent in Turkey on Exercise Anatalion Eagle. During this Exercise, I spent a lot of time out on the line with the lads who were on my shift, trying to learn as much as I could about the aircraft systems. It was a brilliant introduction to both XI Squadron and Typhoon itself. When I returned to RAF Coningsby I was able to hit the ground running.

Being a JENGO is what the training at Cranwell is primarily focused on. The thought processes, academic training and the exercises we do are all geared towards being a Squadron JENGO and the decisions you have to make in such a role – I was very fortunate to get JENGO XI Squadron as my first tour.

My day typically starts at around 07:00hrs; I'll check which jets are serviceable and what the flying programme requires for the day. We'll have an engineering brief at 07:45hrs – from that we can see what is required and what the engineering priorities are. The day is then

LEFT Flying Officer Stephanie Wilde on her posting to Afghanistan.
(Stephanie Wilde)

focused on maintaining the flying programme and dealing with whatever changes to the programme or engineering faults emerge. Typically we'll fly a 4-4-4 flying programme – three waves of four aircraft, either day or night flying. The Squadron is split into two engineering shifts, each ran by a JENGO and Flight Sergeant and comprising mechanical, avionics and weapons technicians. Each shift will do a week on day shift and a week on night shift, with night shift typically being 16:00hrs until 02:00hrs, although the finish time is dictated by the amount of aircraft rectification work ongoing. Being a JENGO can be very reactive; you're constantly making time critical decisions on how to get the most out of the aircraft, meet the flying programme and provide what the pilots need to achieve their training.

I've now been awarded my Typhoon "Reds and Greens", which are the key engineering authorisations an Engineer Officer needs to sign Limitations (LIMS) and Acceptable Deferred Faults (ADF) on the aircraft. It typically takes between three and six months to earn

your Reds and Greens and until this time the Squadron Warrant Officer and Flight Sergeant step in. They will mentor you, along with the Senior Engineer Officer (SENGO), on the aircraft systems and the thought process involved in making key engineering decisions. If it is necessary to raise an ADF or LIM then I will do my own assessment and make a decision based on various different factors.

As a JENGO, you don't work the aircraft yourself or be expected to know every system inside-out. That's what the guys are trained for; they're the system experts and have had the training and hands-on experience. The role of the JENGO is to have an oversight of the broader engineering picture. In terms of job satisfaction, the best thing is when the pilot says "Thank the engineers because that was a sweet jet – everything worked perfectly, the systems were good, I got what I needed for that sortie". That's amazingly satisfying because you see how hard the pilots work, you see how hard the engineers work and when the two produce a result it's a really, really good feeling.'

BELOW Inside a HAS at RAF Coningsby, these RAF technicians check a supersonic fuel tank (SST) (also known as a drop tank). *(Nick Robinson)*

Chief Tech John McCarroll

Chief Tech John McCarroll heads up the avionics trade for his shift on 11 Squadron, reporting to the shift's JENGO. He previously worked on Jaguars and Tornados before being posted to Typhoon.

'I look after avionics on the Typhoon so that's navigation, radar, the attack computer, the Praetorian defensive aids sub-system, the laser designator pod when it's fitted and the flight control system – oh, and displays. So, basically, the whole aircraft really!

'The Typhoon's cutting edge systems have made a huge difference to the working life of the avionics team. You can liken the majority of them to your home computer – if you have a problem with a computer at home, more often than not if you turn it off and restart it, that cures the problem. With the Typhoon having so many computers, it only takes one having a bit of a glitch and you'll hear a phrase "downpower-repower". So that's what the guys do – they'll downpower the aircraft, put power back on and restart it. In nine out of ten cases, that solves the issue.

'From a maintenance point of view, obviously when it comes back there may be software issues so it's often a case of reloading the software. If it's corrupt – the same way that your personal computer software sometimes hangs because the registry is corrupt – a simple reinstallation brings everything back into line.

'There is diagnostic tool that we use – a data bus test set – so we can analyse software on there. Depending on the system, there's a common loading port on the side of the fuselage and we plug straight into there. Generally, it'll be something straightforward like the RAM in the box being corrupt so we'll simply pull it out and replace it. It's that simple.

'We do get more complex faults than that obviously – we've got two fibre-optic lanes with the data bus, lanes A and B on the high-speed, and we've got low-speed buses too.

BELOW Computers are at the heart of the Typhoon's systems. *(RAF)*

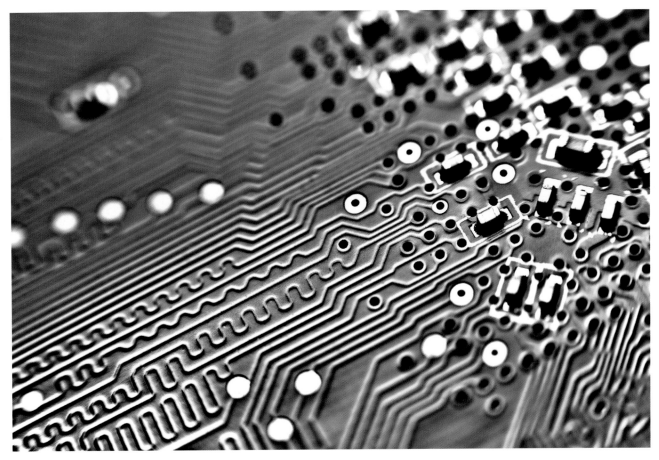

AVTUR
FSII

F-34

PUSH-PULL

Being fibre-optic, they can be quite sensitive to dirt and grease and it only takes a little bit to cause a problem – somebody will take off a plug and rub it, transferring grease from their fingertip or something similarly innocuous. That's caused us a few issues of late but it's easy enough to rectify – there's a cleaning kit we utilise and we also have a viewer that we can use on the fibre-optic cable itself to see if there's any damage on it such as pitting or scarring.

'The only thorn in our side from an engineering perspective at the moment – the dread job I guess you'd call it – is with the DASS. It's refrigerant-based so, before we even think about doing any work on it, we have to decant the refrigerant – weigh it, measure it – and then replace it. That's quite a lengthy task depending on what needs replacing and sometimes, even after you've done all of that, it doesn't actually solve the problem so it can be a real pain in the neck. It's just so time-consuming.

'Also, the ACS [Armament Control System] gives us a few headaches too. Sometimes,

you get an overload on the data bus – it's quite happy with two bombs on an aircraft, but it doesn't like three. Because you're dealing with data buses, it can be something as simple as one of the lanes being down, so too much traffic appears on the other one. Within the software, information has to appear at a specific point at a specific time and if it's not there, the system ignores it. Obviously, the ACS is a critical system – when the pilot selects a bomb or a missile and hits the pickle [bomb release] button or pulls the trigger, he wants something to happen – he's going to have a seriously bad day at work if he presses the button and nothing happens!

'Anything we have to do that involves replacing wires or fibre-optic cables is never going to be a five-minute job so you tend to groan inwardly at the prospect – they're not the sort of jobs you look forward to doing. And of course, given the complexity and densely-packed nature of wiring looms, you can pretty much guarantee that the one you need to replace is right at the heart of the thing. There's not a lot of play on there, so if it's too involved,

it'll go up the line to the "boffins in the building" – the BAE guys on the second-line engineering team – for them to work out a solution. We put in service enquiries and they'll feed back information to us.

'The avionics system – the collection of black boxes which are at the heart of what we do – is located adjacent to the cockpit on the jet but even getting access to it is a pain. There are about 30 screws holding the panel in place which you have to remove before you can even begin to get to work!

'We deal with pretty much everything you see in the cockpit – it all falls under our remit. The HUD, the MHDDs, and to a large degree, everything to do with HOTAS comes down to us, depending on what's wrong. A lot of the functionality on the attack side and the throttle box, too. That said, the MHDDs – most of the kit in the cockpit – are pretty reliable and don't give us too many headaches.

'A good example of the future-proofing of Typhoon can be seen with the HOTAS. Obviously, when the aircraft first came online, it was as a fighter jet, so it was set up in the air-to-air role. But there's a shift button on the HOTAS that allows us to program more functionality to it. So as the aircraft shifted to its multi-role status, that's allowed us to assign additional functions to the buttons and triggers on the stick.

'For all that I've said in terms of negatives about this jet, it has to be seen in perspective because, from an engineering perspective, it's brilliant – peerless, in fact. Compared to my own frame of reference – Jaguar and Tornado – it's of a different class entirely. It makes our job so much easier by comparison, it's almost intuitive. I suppose I'd liken it to a contemporary car – you've got fingertip remote control for the in-car entertainment system on the steering wheel, head-up displays, adaptive headlights, intelligent monitoring systems that dial 999 if you're involved in a crash, TV screens and internet, and reversing cameras. Contrast that with something like a high-end BMW or Mercedes from 30 years ago and the most technologically-advanced element would have been an automated choke. That's the Typhoon compared with the Tornado.'

ABOVE Avionics technician in the cockpit. *(Nick Robinson)*

ABOVE AND ABOVE RIGHT The Martin-Baker Mk 16a ejection seat is the most advanced escape system ever made. *(Nick Robinson/Antony Loveless)*

RIGHT Maintenance and engineering scheduler. *(Nick Robinson)*

Chief Tech Jonathan Salt

Chief Tech Jonathan Salt is 11 Squadron's Weapons Trade Manager. Prior to Typhoon, he worked on Jaguar, Tornado and Harrier squadrons.

'The weapons trade is responsible for all weapons that are currently available to the Typhoon – bombs, missiles and guns. My trade also includes the escape systems, so the Mk 16a ejection seat and all associated equipment also falls under my remit.

'The Mk 16a is an amazing piece of kit, the most advanced seat that Martin Baker has ever produced – but it sounds so trite to call it a mere seat. It's effectively an escape system. The guys learn about it as part of their trade training – they learn a basic understanding of ejection systems at RAF Cosford. That's added to during their weapons Q course at RAF Coningsby and the final stage is annual training to ensure that they're still safe and cognisant of all relevant procedures and safety requirements.

'At squadron level, we're involved in everything from the removal to the installation of the equipment from the aircraft. That includes the removal of the canopy through to the actual seat coming out. We change the seat's cartridge and numerous base-level components such as the arm restraint lines and leg lines.

'The Mk 16a is a far more intricate system than the Mk 9s, 10s and 12s that were fitted in the Jaguars, Harriers and Tornados. These, while not "simple systems", were very mechanically driven. That meant there were specific timing parameters so everything worked in a standard sequence, everything was controlled mechanically. The Mk 16a is digital rather than analogue and represents a step change in development. It actually controls when and how to release the pilot from the ejection seat based on pre-programmed parameters. It still has the same characteristics as any other seat in that, in an absolute situation, it will come out of the aeroplane and release him, but additionally, it can actually retain him in the seat to keep him safe until the parameters are met.

'In terms of other responsibilities, we look after all of the Typhoon's role equipment so that would include the pylons, the gun system and the external fuel tanks – the supersonic ones, which are 1,000kg each. We look after the flare system and we also have links into the ACS, or Armament Control System, although the lead is with the avionics trade for that.'

TYPHOON'S SELF-DIAGNOSIS AND REPORTING

Most of the problems facing the engineers on a daily basis are avionics-based but the Typhoon's self-diagnostic system gives the RAF's technicians easy access to any data determining the jet's maintenance status. There are two routes open to them in identifying problems.

One of them is the maintenance data panel, which is built into the Typhoon's fuselage. This allows the engineers to look through and analyse all of the aircraft's systems. Secondly, the aircraft utilises a Portable Maintenance Data Storage (PMDS) device which isn't that different from a conventional removable hard drive. Known colloquially as 'the brick', this enables the engineers to download data covering the aircraft's flight details and maintenance status to an information management system known as the Engineering Support System (ESS). After every sortie, the engineers remove the PDMS and download its data to the ESS. Over time, this paints a picture of every aspect of the jet and its flying history that can be analysed in detail. They can look back through each aircraft's history and see at a glance if any individual component is showing signs of degradation or stress.

ESS allows the engineers to assess every aspect of each Typhoon's serviceability, systems and engines, giving them information on a diverse range of data covering everything from engine operating limits to G-loading on the airframe. Diagnosis of any potential problems can be made quickly, giving the ground crew a heads up before they manifest themselves to the pilot.

Chapter Seven

Typhoon in service

'The first time I engaged weapons on a sortie was against a couple of BTR60 APCs in a Libyan forest. We were talked on to them – I was with a GR4 in a pair so we rolled out and had a look and we both hit them with a couple of Enhanced Paveway IIs.'
Flight Lieutenant Nick Graham, pilot, 3 Squadron

OPPOSITE An RAF Typhoon on a mission during Operation Ellamy (Libya), showing the Enhanced Paveway II bombs plus an air-to-air AMRAAM missile. *(RAF)*

The Falkland Islands

Mount Pleasant is a British tri-service garrison located 35 miles from Port Stanley in the Falkland Islands, and is home to over 2,000 personnel charged with defending Britain's sovereignty over her interests in the South Atlantic. There has been a permanent British presence in the Falklands since 1833 and, from a legal perspective, the Islands are an overseas territory of the United Kingdom. As such, the Falklands Government relies on the UK to guarantee their security. The other UK territories in the South Atlantic – South Georgia and the South Sandwich Islands – also fall under the protection of the British forces on the Falklands.

The maintenance of only a token military force of just 100 or so Royal Marines before the Falklands War of 1982 was no match for the Argentinean military and the islands were quickly captured. Following the Task Force's success in the battle to retake the Falklands (Operation Corporate), the UK invested heavily in the defence of the Islands, the centre-piece of which is Mount Pleasant, which opened in 1985 to replace the previous base at Port Stanley. As such, it is the Royal Air Force's most

recently built base, the majority of those in the UK dating from 1931.

The first thing you notice upon arriving in the Falklands is the light; it's of a clarity and brightness quite unlike that found anywhere else in the world. With the atmosphere devoid of dust and pollutants, what your eyes have is pure, perfect vision. Sparkling night skies, unspoilt by light pollution from major conurbations, enhance the naturally bright vista of the southern hemisphere. This clarity comes from a combination of the Islands' location so far south – Port Stanley is the world's southernmost city – and the Islands' tiny population. Covering a geographical area roughly approximate to Wales, the Falkland Islanders number just 2,400, with almost 2,000 of those living in the capital, Stanley – a city comparable in size and population to the average British hamlet! In addition, the location of the Falkland Islands – just 900 miles from Antarctica and some way distant from any major centres of population – contributes to the outstanding clarity of the light.

The second thing that you notice, especially if you're a first-time visitor to the Mount Pleasant airbase arriving by air, is a brace of RAF Typhoons, one stationed off each wing-

BELOW No 1435 Flight Typhoon flying over the Falkland Islands on 13 August 2010. *(RAF)*

tip, from about 200 miles and 10,000ft out. They're there for every flight both inbound and outbound, escorting commercial airliners down to the ground or away to their destinations. But this is no MoD PR exercise designed to entertain awe-struck passengers; it's the most graphic reminder of exactly why Britain's forces are stationed in this South Atlantic outpost, 8,000 miles and 18 hours from home.

There are four Typhoons stationed on the Falklands, their crews drawn from the UK's four permanent Typhoon squadrons. Whilst stationed in the Falklands, they form 1435 Flight, the Islands' resident defence squadron. All RAF fighter pilots in the UK are cycled through 1435 Flight, the only limitation being that they possess the necessary weather flying qualifications. They each serve tours of four weeks and can expect to return roughly three times a year throughout their service.

The aircraft that form 1435 Flight have traditionally been known as *Faith, Hope, Charity*

(as were the three Gloster Gladiators of 1435 Flight when it defended Malta in the early years of the Second World War) and *Desperation*. The Flight maintained its Maltese connections right up to 2009, when its Tornado F3 aircraft sported the Maltese Cross. In September of that year, the Tornados were replaced with the current four Typhoon FGR2s. Although these don't have the traditional names applied, nor do they sport the Maltese Cross, the four aircraft have tail codes that match (F, H, C, D) in an affectionate nod to the past.

The deployment of the four Typhoons that replaced the F3s to form 1435 Flight involved a logistical task of Herculean proportions. Five aircraft – ZJ944, ZJ945, ZJ949, ZJ950 and ZK301 – departed for the Falkland Islands on 12 September 2009. The deployment required a total of ten support aircraft from four squadrons flying a total of 280 hours and supported by some 95 personnel, in addition to the fighters and their aircrews.

ABOVE A Typhoon of 1435 Flight in QRA fit breaks away from the camera. Slats and flaperons are deployed while the foreplanes maintain stability. *(RAF)*

Flight Typhoon's tail markings. *(RAF)*

The aircraft were accompanied to Ascension Island by VC10 tankers from 101 Squadron in a two-stage operation that used the Canary Islands as a staging post en-route to the Falklands. RAF Hercules and Nimrod aircraft provided Search and Rescue cover for the long sea transits, and were stocked with survival equipment and spare life rafts that could be dropped to any survivors in the water in the event of an incident that necessitated an ejection.

In all, each Typhoon was required to refuel seven times. There's a VC10 tanker permanently stationed in the Falklands and that was on hand to provide a final top-up if required. It also provided insurance in that its fuel would have enabled the Typhoons to divert to South America had the weather deteriorated unexpectedly during the nine-and-a-half hour transit.

The Typhoons arrived at Mount Pleasant on 16 September. ZJ945 subsequently returned to RAF Coningsby, leaving the other aircraft at Britain's southernmost base. So why are they there?

The UK government spends at least £80m a year to run the Falkland Islands' defences, roughly equivalent to Argentina's entire annual military budget. And those charged with the Islands' defence number almost as many as those resident there. But if islanders no longer live in fear of Argentina's military intentions, that does not mean the future is necessarily assured, hence the establishment of forces at Mount Pleasant.

These assets in theatre are no paper tiger, either; despite Argentina's failing economy and the stated aim of its government to pursue sovereignty claims through diplomatic channels only, the Typhoons are regularly scrambled to warn off Argentine ships and aircraft testing the response to threats against the 150-mile exclusion zone.

No 1435 Flight is the most visceral element of this policy – the British government's tip of the spear, there to protect sovereignty of the Falklands and neighbouring territories against any perceived threat. With Argentina still pressing its claim for ownership – and memories of Galtieri's attempt to seize the islands through force still raw – 1435's four Typhoons are a visible and practical deterrent to any repeat of such short-sighted plans. And it wouldn't take long to fly in reinforcements, should they be required.

Mount Pleasant's main runway – said to be wider than most to cope with the frequent strong cross-winds – is an important element of the Islands' defences. Reinforcements could be flown in at short notice via Ascension Island, which is positioned conveniently almost half-way between the UK and the Falklands. But, if needs be, the RAF could fly transport aircraft to Mount Pleasant non-stop, refuelling in mid-air.

There's another benefit to Britain's armed forces in having the unrivalled facilities presented by the Falkland Islands in terms of training. Quite simply there is nowhere else on earth that offers the same ability for our forces to practise. Be it the army on live firing exercises, or practise intercepts against slow-moving targets and low-level attacks by 1435 Flight's Typhoons, there's nowhere else with the geography and sparse population of the Falkland Islands. It's all in uncontrolled airspace with no over-flying traffic, perfect for honing low-level flying ability, a vital skill for fighter pilots which goes off very quickly unless used constantly. That's something that just isn't possible within the UK.

Perhaps the best illustration of the benefits afforded by the Falklands in training terms comes from contemporary news. When you see reports of commercial passenger jets with suspect packages aboard, or errant helicopters being intercepted by Typhoons scrambled from RAF Coningsby or RAF Leuchars, you're witnessing the skills honed in the Falkland

Islands. The average commercial passenger flying away on holiday is likely to be a little disturbed, to put it mildly, by the sight of fighter jets shadowing their flight, but Britain's fighter pilots need somewhere they can practice for a skill that they are increasingly being called upon to exercise post 9/11. The airspace surrounding the Falklands is that place.

Where else are the pilots and their controllers on the ground going to rehearse the finer points of vectoring a £65m fighter jet alongside a fully loaded commercial airliner? It's written into the contract that the Ministry of Defence awards airlines providing the airbridge to the Falklands that the RAF's fighters may practice intercepts of flights to Mount Pleasant.

And given the small geographical footprint of Mount Pleasant airbase, nowhere else features such a broad collection of military personnel and assets. Fighter controllers can vector the Typhoons against helicopters, passenger jets or slow-moving light aircraft. The Hercules can make low level drops onto the airfield, whilst the resident Rapier defences attempt to track and 'kill' the aircraft. And afterwards, those involved can all debrief the day's events together.

Put simply, the Falkland Islands offer Britain's military an unrivalled opportunity to train and hone their vital skills whilst at the same time protecting one of Britain's last remaining territories. You can't put a price on that.

BELOW Three Typhoons of 1435 Flight over the Falkland Islands. *(RAF)*

Operation Ellamy

Typhoon's first blood

On 17 February 2011, with the Arab Spring providing the backdrop, Colonel Muammar Gaddafi began using military force to quell unrest among his own people. As the violence escalated, the UK evacuated foreign and UK nationals from Libya under the aegis of Operation Deference.

At a meeting of the United Nations Security Council early in the evening of 17 March 2011 a new Resolution – 1973 – was proposed by France, Lebanon, and the United Kingdom. The resolution formed the legal basis for military intervention in the Libyan civil war, demanding 'an immediate ceasefire' and authorising the international community to establish a no-fly zone and to use 'all means necessary short of foreign occupation to protect civilians'.

Ten Security Council members voted in the affirmative, five abstained, with none opposed and Resolution 1973 was duly passed.

Later that night at 22:00hrs, Group Captain Sammy Sampson, the station commander of RAF Coningsby, was interrupted at a dining-in night at the officers' mess. Back in his office, he received a phone call from HQ Air Command with orders to prepare Typhoons for a potential deployment. By late afternoon just two days later – on Saturday 19 March – 12 XI Squadron

Typhoons were standing by for deployment, fully loaded and combat ready.

That in itself was no easy task – the jets had to be taken out of training and readied for a direct operational environment, which involved 3 (F) Squadron and 29 (R) Squadron personnel preparing them. Ordinarily, it would take the station three to four days to prepare just one aircraft for ops. In the event, they prepared 12 aircraft in only 36 hours, a genuinely superhuman effort. And while XI Squadron would be leading from an aircraft and engineering aspect, on the flying side it was most definitely a wing effort, with pilots from both 3 (F) and 29 (R) Squadrons involved.

From a Ministry of Defence perspective, the Typhoon was the perfect aircraft for the job. The jets were involved in QRA (Quick Reaction Alert) so they were already configured for air defence – it would just be a case of protecting a different piece of airspace. Gioia del Colle in Southern Italy was selected as the base for deployment and when the call came at 10:30hrs on Sunday 20 March, the Typhoons and their crews were ready and waiting. They were airborne and on their way by 13:00hrs. Group Captain Sampson flew out later that afternoon as commander of the Expeditionary Air Wing (EAW) which also required a headquarters element of 19 personnel to be mobilised. They arrived in Gioia along with some 31 ground crew about three hours after the Typhoons touched down.

It was immediately apparent on arriving that they'd need to get airborne urgently. Whilst the air threat in terms of Libyan aircraft was all but non-existent, the threat to the Libyan people was real and immediate. The first Typhoons were launched to enforce the no-fly zone within 24 hours of arrival on the Monday morning.

The Libyan Air Force may have been neutered but the RAF pilots flying sorties over Libya soon realised that a significant threat to them existed in the form of anti-aircraft defences, active radar-guided Surface-to-Air Missiles (SAM) and Anti-Aircraft Artillery (AAA). And although the Typhoon is equipped with an extensive Defensive Aids Sub-System (DASS), it was untried in combat. Any concerns were soon set aside as the DASS proved itself worthy.

The Typhoons were tasked with a variety of missions and, although initially they flew sorties

BELOW A Typhoon is prepared at RAF Coningsby prior to take-off in support of United Nations Resolution 1973 to enforce the Libya no-fly zone. *(RAF)*

in pairs, they quickly began flying as mixed pairs with Tornado GR4s. Gaddafi's forces were attacking the civilian population, Misrata was under siege, there was a lot of activity in the centre of the capital city Tripoli, and there were a lot of airfields across the country with assets on them that could be turned upon the Libyan people. Logistically, it was a challenge flying combat air patrols, especially given that nine-tenths of the population lived along a coastline some 600 to 800km long.

In addition, the Typhoon pilots had to be prepared to protect the assets supporting them – tankers, AWACS and other Coalition aircraft. It was exactly this mix of missions that the Typhoons were suited to; they often operated over three separate areas spread over 800km in a single sortie.

With the battlefront spread over such a wide geographic area and numerous Coalition aircraft airborne at any given time, pilots of previous generation fighters may have been overwhelmed by the complexity of the air picture with which

they were confronted. Here though, the Typhoon really played to its strengths.

As Group Captain Sampson says:

'The Typhoon provides amazing situational awareness, through MIDS [Multifunctional Information Distribution System], the radar, its communications suite and its ability to integrate with other assets. We had NATO and Coalition airborne command and control assets, but, in particular, we worked very closely with UK AWACS, Nimrod R1 and Sentinel. Whenever we came up with that combination – it wasn't engineered, but it happened – it was particularly potent. Typhoon is able to take information from all those sensors and Coalition aircraft and sensors, and fuse it and present it in a useful way to the pilot. We have fantastic displays and the jet is thoroughly optimised for single-seat combat. We don't have to constantly check the health of the aeroplane and its systems allowing real mission focus. If you look at the Libya situation, it was very complex in the air, very complicated and ambiguous on the ground and

ABOVE A Typhoon of 3 (F) Squadron takes off from RAF Coningsby to take part in the UN-backed operation over Libya. *(RAF)*

ABOVE **Typhoon FGR4 taking off from Gioia del Colle with Enhanced Paveway II, Litening III pod, and air-to-air ASRAAM missiles.** *(RAF)*

where Typhoon came into its own is that there was no complexity in the cockpit. The aeroplane is designed to take that complexity away so the majority task is to resolve complexity in the battlespace, not within the cockpit.

'It became clear fairly early on that there would be no air-to-air threat for the Typhoon pilots to counter, so the aircraft were quickly re-roled for air-to-ground work, armed with Raytheon Enhanced Paveway II laser-GPS-guided bombs and equipped with the Litening III targeting pod.

'The way Typhoon's systems are integrated, it doesn't matter if you're on an air-to-surface profile. The radar is still there, the information doesn't go away, it's still being presented in a way that adds to your capabilities. We can maintain a very credible, potent air-to-air capability while conducting other missions whether flying as wingman for a Tornado GR4 or another Typhoon, conducting C-ISTAR, or as part of an air-to-surface capability. The air-to-air capability is always able to be "tuned" up or down, sat in the background ready to be called on very quickly.'

Back at RAF Coningsby, 3 (F) Squadron were making plans to take over the mantle from XI Squadron at Gioia. Led by Wing Commander 'Dicky' Patounas, they'd had three months to prepare so were in good shape when they arrived. Their timing was immaculate –

their deployment happened to coincide with the busiest and most kinetic period of the whole operation. They had fewer aircraft – XI Squadron started with twelve and ended up with six. 3 (F) Squadron started with six and ended with four. Both squadrons flew almost exactly the same number of hours – some 1500 – over the same period. They had 99% serviceability and when they were down to only a few aircraft, each was flying 100 hours per month. Back home at RAF Coningsby, they fly an average of 20–25 hours.

It was a baptism of fire, with pilots regularly flying six-and-a-half-hour missions. They were also involved in pre-planned missions whereby they were taking part in large packages. As Dicky Patounas says, 'You'd fly as a four-ship element within a larger number of four-ships so there might be 32 or 36 aircraft in a "gorilla" package. That'd be a coordinated package providing defensive counter air, suppression of enemy air defences, and providing bombs of the sizes and shapes that there are in the Coalition to have the desired effect.'

Fortunately, XI Squadron had done a great job of setting up what was initially a very austere base so it was much more comfortable and significantly better established for the newly-arrived crews. Dicky Patounas details here a typical sortie that he was involved in on Operation Ellamy:

'On every sortie, we crossed the Med before we even started. Then we would go 300 miles plus inland. Very occasionally, the guys would go beyond the joint personnel recovery line, deeper than they could be recovered. So they put themselves in a potentially risky situation – carefully calculated versus the imperative but some brave stuff nonetheless.

'On my second-to-last mission I was tasked to Bani Walid with a Tornado. To the south of the city I found a tank dug in by a checkpoint. By the checkpoint were some people – my bomb was too big, so we used the GR4's Brimstone and destroyed the tank.

'We were then tasked to Sirte because there were some main battle tanks firing. By then it was dark and it turned out that the locals had fireworks going off. I suspect that the firing was spotted by the maritime fleet and they couldn't tell that the flashes were fireworks. We watched

the fireworks for an hour and established that they were civilians doing whatever they were doing – I don't know why they had fireworks! Then they tasked us down to Waddan. There were two MRLs [Multiple Rocket Launchers] and two Technicals causing a lot of damage to some civilians so we destroyed the vehicles and then went home.

'That was seven-and-a-quarter hours. To put the geographic scale of what we did into context, we effectively took off in Oslo and our first task took us to London. We spent an hour over London finding and destroying a tank without hurting anybody. We were then tasked to Paris, where we watched fireworks for an hour. Then we were tasked to Luxembourg, where we destroyed four vehicles, before returning to Oslo. That shows you the reach, responsiveness and precision of air power. Everything that combat air power represents was in those sorties. And that was just daily business. It included four trips to the tanker – I arrived, filled up with gas, did my Bani Walid task, filled up again, did my Sirte task, filled up again, did my Waddan task, had a further splash of gas, and then made a dash home.

'All the refuelling was done over the sea, in various locations, remembering that Libya is 500 miles along its coast. Sometimes you rock up with not a lot of gas and the tanker's not there, or has a problem and can't give you fuel, and so

it gets quite interesting. There's no way you want to let the fuel get "in the red" and hope there'll be a tanker along soon, not in a low-risk war. If it was the Battle of Britain we'd do anything for Queen and country but, with the guidelines we were given, we always had enough to find a safe haven if the tanker didn't work.'

Overall, the combination of Typhoon, ISTAR and hi-tech weapons introduced the RAF into a new world, even compared with Operation Iraqi Freedom in 2003. Typhoon proved that it could provide battle-winning information, allowing operations at a rapid tempo with an accuracy that was previously impossible. Dicky Patounas provides an example:

'I flew Jaguars from Gioia 15 years ago and went north instead of south. Allied Force [the Kosovo campaign] and Unified Protector are two fundamentally different wars, although, arguably, we were doing much the same thing. But we couldn't do any of this 15 years ago. We were good with what we had but this is *Star Wars* by comparison. The awareness I have in the Typhoon versus the Jaguar is not comparable.

'I've never had an easier aeroplane to fly in my life, but it can really bite you because there's so much going on in there that you can get distracted. You need to be on top of your game all of the time. The rate of wrongness can increase very quickly!'

ABOVE No 11 Squadron FGR4 in air policing fit armed with AMRAAM and ASRAAM missiles takes off from Gioia de Colle on 28 March 2011. *(RAF)*

Flight Lieutenant Nick Graham

At the time of Operation Ellamy, Nick Graham was a front-line pilot with 3(F) Squadron.

'I was deployed on Operation Ellamy in the second wave. I remember the night we found out – we had a dining-in night in the mess and the station commander stood on the table and said, "Everyone go home and sober up, I'll see you all in the morning. We're going to war."

'It was June when I deployed – I strapped into a Typhoon late one night and landed in Italy about 02:00hrs and that was it. It was obvious the minute I arrived at the ops room that this was the real deal and not a training environment. Maps were covered up, there was a guard on the door and there was an armoury where guys were drawing pistols. I got myself a room at the hotel where we were accommodated and crashed out.

'A lot of the fighting was between mercenaries working for Gaddafi and the Libyan people who were trying to take back their country. We knew the mercenaries were coming from the Sub-Saharan Desert and heading north through a series of staging posts and we had intelligence indicating where these staging posts were and what they were being used for. We were particularly interested in the last one, which appeared to be the final jumping off-point for them so they were all tooled up with weapons and equipment there. These guys were doing some really horrific things and we were tasked with doing something about it.

'It was about 02:00hrs when we took off on this particular sortie so it was very dark and we had about 600 miles to fly to where we needed to be. I was flying in a two-ship and my wingman was in a Tornado so, as the GR4s couldn't fly as high or as fast as us, they'd take off first. We'd launch as a singleton some time later and go over the top of them and we'd rendezvous at a tanker to take on fuel.

'On this particular mission our Typhoons were loaded with four Enhanced PaveWays (EPW) each plus AMRAAMs and ASRAAMs plus a targeting pod – that's an awful lot of explosive when you think about it. We went as a four-ship comprising two Typhoons, each with a wingman in a GR4. The two GR4s went off first, and we flew over the top of them and met up at the tanker. On the way out, we were on NVGs [Night-Vision Goggles] and we flew over Mount Etna which was erupting at the time so that was pretty special. Because of the warm air coming up off the mountains, you'd get the most enormous thunderstorms which would go right up through the tropopause, all the way to 40,000ft and beyond. Looking through the NVGs, you wouldn't see the clouds until lightning lit them up from inside and it was the most incredible spectacle.

'On the downside, they were incredibly ferocious – one of the Tornado guys had a really lucky escape as he was coming down through a cloud which happened to have a thunderstorm embedded and it turned his aircraft into a golf ball, literally left big dents and holes in it. He was carrying a Brimstone underneath and the lens on the front of the bomb was completely smashed. Brimstone has a direct fusing plate on the front, so if another

chunk of hail had hit it, it could have been very nasty indeed.

'Anyway, we took some fuel onboard from a US KC-10 tanker and then flew on as a Typhoon pair to the location we'd been given, which was essentially a farmer's hut. We had good intelligence that there were an awful lot of bad guys in there so we flew over the target and hit it with eight Paveways. By the time we'd completed that element of the mission, the sun was coming up and we needed more fuel so we went back to the tanker and loaded up again before flying back to where we'd dropped the bombs so we could conduct a BDA [Battle Damage Assessment]. As you might imagine, there was nothing left of the target, and no survivors.

'On that mission both Typhoons were carrying Litening Pods so we had both been using them to look into the target area, making sure that we were clear to engage under current rules of engagement. That's one of the reasons that we chose to make the attack at that time

of the morning – if there's anyone around that early at that location, it's highly unlikely they're innocent civilians going about their business. We flew over at about 22,000ft at about 0.8 Mach with the Litening Pods trained on the target so we had eyes on and then we committed the weapons. To do that, you create a waypoint which you designate as the target and assign a weapons package to it. The computers do the rest. There's a flap on top of the control stick which you flip open with your thumb and then you simply hit the pickle button to send the weapons you've selected to the target you've identified. Job done.

'The work load is quite high on the run in. There's a lot of button-pushing and entering of coordinates to input the targets, assign weapons, etc as the system's still relatively austere. Bear in mind you're trying to do all this while you're flying at eight miles per minute so there's no time for the big moral questions – you know, "Oh, I wonder what's going on down there, what are they thinking, etc."

RIGHT Operation Ellamy, an armed Typhoon on a wet dispersal. *(RAF)*

Dateline 23 March 2011. No XI Squadron Typhoons deployed on Operation Ellamy wait on the pan at Gioia del Colle Air Base, Italy. Ellamy saw RAF Typhoons used in anger for the first time. *(RAF)*

'It's pretty impressive when you do it during the day – you hit the button, there's an almost imperceptible delay while the computer works out what it's supposed to be doing and then there's a sort of shudder from the aircraft as the first two bombs are released – bear in mind that as they drop, that's two tonnes of weight you've just shed, so suddenly the aircraft feels a lot lighter. And as they drop, you can look over the side of the cockpit and see them directly below you, tracking forwards at the same speed as the aircraft. On the Typhoon, the foreplanes sit forward of your knee, and the wing is way back behind you, so if you look over the side, you can see straight down.

'The first weapon I saw deployed was from my wingman in a GR4 on one of my first sorties in theatre. We'd spent several hours on a patrol over this particular area, we were low on fuel and about to turn for home when the Tornado saw some tanks which he engaged with a Brimstone. That was pretty impressive to watch as I was just alongside. It's hard to believe the damage those Brimstones do, especially given their relatively small size – it was like watching a firework go off! My job was to scan the area to make sure that nothing else was coming towards the target so I had it covered with my pod and I watched the Brimstone cook off and drop down to the lower levels, tracking it as it went. I watched the tank on one of my screens as the pod scanned the area and saw the Brimstone as it struck home. That was impressive.

'One of the problems with Brimstone is that it's incredibly accurate but you can't always tell from height what damage it's caused. They tend to hit hard on armour and the kinetic energy is transferred through to the inside, killing everyone inside but leaving the outside pretty much unscathed. So unless you see the munition hit, it's often hard to tell if it's actually done any damage.

'Anyway, after the sortie we turned for home – separately, because of the difference in performance – so I was up at 40,000ft for the transit back to Gioia. You switch from the military side of air traffic control for that and go straight to Malta radar control with all the Ryanairs, BAs, Alitalias and Easyjets and it's really weird to think that they're full of people off on their holidays and we're on our way back from war but sharing the same air traffic control. The two elements are so incongruous, the dichotomy so great – you almost imagine there must be some wall between the two so the different worlds don't collide but you get that sense of "disconnect".

'There's talk of "the morality of altitude". It's a term that was coined to apply to bomber pilots who release their payloads on victims they can't see, without ever feeling any sense of remorse

or empathy for the people whose lives, families, homes and property they destroy. I think it's unfair to apply it to us. The targeting pod is a complete game-changer in that regard because it puts you up close and personal with the effects of your weapons. In many respects, we see clearer and closer when we engage and get weapons on than infantry soldiers when they do. Once upon a time it was only snipers who saw the damage their rounds did first hand but technology has brought the same thing to pilots flying at 20,000ft.

'What it means is you don't just turn up at the target, drop your bombs and fly home for tea and crumpets. We spend ages flying over the target, watching, making sure and double-checking that the intelligence is correct, and that there aren't any civilians in proximity. You have a huge weight of legal responsibility on

your shoulders and you are constantly aware of the rules of engagement, which can be massively complicated. Then there's your choice of weapon, which has to be appropriate for the target. You can't go blithely dropping a 1,000lb bomb to take out a single nasty individual who might be in a market place because the effects of that weapon are so widespread. If you haven't got a point-to-point weapon that will take him out without collateral damage, you don't engage. Ultimately, it's about using the right tool for the job.

'You don't want to screw it up because, morality and philosophical angles aside, you would have a huge amount of trouble personally – like going to prison for the rest of your life. All of that makes a pretty strong argument for getting it right, every single time.

'The first time I engaged weapons on a

ABOVE An RAF Typhoon FGR4 takes off for Libya from Gioia del Colle carrying four 1,000lb Enhanced PaveWay II (EPW II) bombs, Litening III targeting pod, AMRAAM and ASRAAM. *(RAF)*

sortie was against a couple of BTR60 Armoured Personnel Carriers [APCs] which were in a forest. Talk about confound your expectations – I'd imagined Libya would be all desert with a lot of coast but like I say, these two APCs were in a forest. We'd had intelligence that they'd been going out in the night and doing some really nasty stuff to the local population – rolling into town, hosing them down with their heavy machine guns and then retreating back under darkness to hide out in the forest.

'We were talked on to them – I was with a GR4 in a pair so we rolled out and had a look and we both hit them with a couple of EPW IIs [Enhanced Paveway II]. We were pretty low on fuel so turned back and headed for the tanker, then went back to the forest and engaged the other BTR60. There wasn't a lot left of either of them when we'd finished.

'I can remember another daytime mission. It was a Toyota Hi-Lux of all things, with a .50 cal on the back, one of those Technicals – the terrorists' friend. They were engaging some rebels but they were a good mile, or a mile-and-a-half away from them in the desert and there was a single tree that they'd parked up behind which effectively masked them from the rebels' view. But from the air it looked bonkers because you could see for miles around and there was nothing on the landscape except this lone tree they were parked behind and a mile or so away from them were the rebels who were taking a pounding from them.

'It was all about matching the right weapon to the problem and in this case I used an EPW II for no other reason than they cost a lot less than anything the Tornado carried. Given the space the Technical had around it, there wasn't exactly any danger of collateral damage from the weapon. The Paveways are dead-on accurate and I scored a direct hit on the Toyota.

'Everything you hang from the jet impacts its performance in some way. I don't just mean in terms of the impact all the extra weight has on its performance, so it feels a little less flighty and eager than when it's clean. I mean, the load out on a typical sortie on Ellamy would have seen me carrying four bombs, a targeting pod, two 1,000-litre fuel tanks, two AMRAAMs, two ASRAAMs... that's a hell of a lot of extra weight.

'The targeting pod for instance gives you a bit of an altitude cap because the higher you go, the less cooling air is directed over it so you have to think carefully about how high you're going to go. That in turn affects your fuel profile [higher is better because the air is less dense which means the aircraft flies with less drag, therefore it uses less fuel]. You also notice an effect on the roll rate – you move the stick hard over to the side and the jet just takes a nanosecond longer to move; you let go of the stick and it stops a tiny bit slower.

'You don't really notice it in pure power terms so much – in a normal launch, we'll lift on dry heat only. With weapons on, we engage reheat and the power is exactly the same so it doesn't feel any different. Amazing when you think of it in those terms really, it just has so much grunt.

'That said, reheat on any fighter gives it a really dipsomaniac thirst. If I'm cruising at height I'll burn less than if I'm at low level on reheat, or during dog-fighting.

'So we only use reheat if it's necessary – to get airborne on a performance take-off for example. We use it on the OCU to demonstrate air combat manoeuvres and show students just what a difference it makes. We'll take off on reheat and go nose up at 60 or 70 degrees and we'll say to the student, "Alright fella, if you look over your shoulder and see how far we're travelling over the ground – it's nothing really. Now look how high and fast we're climbing. Now if another fighter can't do that, he's going to be travelling over the ground while you're climbing above him which gives you the vital separation to get your weapons on him. He can't touch you because he can't get front-on to you and he's going to fly out in front of you where it's game over." That's all down to the Typhoon's ferocious power – it's truly phenomenal.

'Flying back from some of the missions over Libya was always interesting but never more so than on the occasions when we were supporting another jet with our Litening pods. On those missions, we didn't carry any bombs so we'd fly with just an air-to-air weapons fit. I'd climb to 50-odd thousand feet at 1.6 Mach for 600 miles, all the way home. And the best bit is, we get paid to do that!

'When I was on the F3, we had an operating

ceiling of about 25,000ft max so when the weather was really ropey you were hamstrung – as soon as you reached the ceiling that was it, game over. In the Typhoon there are no such limitations because we can climb and get above the weather – we can go above the tropopause and into the stratosphere. That's all because of the engines and the brilliant flight control system. As far as that translates tactically, the faster and the higher we can go before we pull the trigger means the more energy there is on that missile – kinetic and potential. That means it will go further and when it goes further and gets to the target, it still has an excess of energy on it. That means we can reach out and touch people before they can do anything to us – before they even know we're there. It's not just based on the missile's capability, a lot has to do with the launch platform.

'I flew roughly 15 or 16 combat sorties over the two months we were in theatre and they averaged something like six or seven hours each so it was pretty high intensity. Looking back though, one of the things that stands out

is just how well the Typhoon proved its edge. To do all that we did in Libya – carrying both an air-to-air fit and all those bombs we had – you'd have needed four F-16s to do what just one Typhoon did. That's how good it is. That's its edge.

'I've flown the aircraft clean a few times – that's how we had them when we flew to RAF Northolt to take up QRA for London 2012 – and it's utterly bonkers. You can supercruise in it with a centreline fuel tank hanging off the fuselage but without that, with nothing whatsoever hung off the mounting points, the sheer power, the thrust, is off the deep end. I've done a couple of performance sorties like that so you take off on reheat and keep it on. You fly some supersonic manoeuvres so you're doing barrel rolls in the contrails. You're up where airliners are on the ropey edge of flying/not flying and you're doing barrel rolls at 1.3 Mach and looking over your shoulder at the corkscrew contrails you're painting across the sky. Like I said – bonkers!

'It's not a bad day at the office, I have to say.'

BELOW No 11 Squadron Typhoon take-off, Operation Ellamy, 11 April 2011. *(RAF)*

Chapter Eight

QRA Typhoon

'Within minutes of the call to scramble the Typhoons are airborne, the ground falling away as they climb and accelerate to meet whatever in-bound threat has been assessed a danger to British airspace. Their first task is to get alongside a suspect aircraft, and become the eyes of the decision maker. Then, if needed, they are his finger on the trigger.'

OPPOSITE No 3 (F) Squadron ground crew run to a Typhoon during a QRA exercise at RAF Coningsby. While final checks are carried out to release the aircraft, the pilot runs to his Typhoon F2 which has been 'cocked' ready for engine start. *(Geoff Lee/Eurofighter)*

Britain's Quick Reaction Alert (QRA) system

A statement in 2007 by the then-head of MI5, The Security Service, Dame Eliza Mannigham-Buller, underlined the extent of the current terrorist threat facing Britain. Her statement – and the London 2012 Olympic Games – reinforced the threat of high-profile strikes by al-Qaeda and once again raised the spectre of bomb-laden passenger jets flying over London's skies.

The 2006 plot by three British Muslims to carry out a series of coordinated suicide bomb attacks on transatlantic airliners between Heathrow and the US could have killed up to 10,000 people. That and 9/11 both showed that using commercial aircraft as weapons of mass destruction is an al-Qaeda trademark. But how can Britain counter such a threat? Since 9/11, shooting down hijacked commercial airliners has been the stark option facing those in the front line of Britain's war on terror. Whilst we go about our daily business, the RAF's fighter pilots live with our nightmares.

It was the events of 9/11 that forced the RAF to look at how it would counter so-called 'asymmetric threats' from terrorist groups using civilian airliners as weapons of mass destruction. The original burden of this new mission profile fell upon the Tornado F3 force maintaining Quick Reaction Alert (QRA).

QRA has been in place since the days of the cold war. Its brief is to detect, deter and, if necessary, intercept and destroy any aircraft which pose a threat to Britain's airspace

Today's QRA comprises armed Typhoon FGR4s held at ground readiness for immediate take-off together with an Air Surveillance/Control System to provide command and control of the jets, and tanker aircraft also held at high ground readiness. The Typhoons are weapons of last resort, fed by intelligence and backed up by a huge counter-terrorism operation on the ground.

To provide geographic coverage, there are two aircraft continuously on QRA at RAF Leuchars (covering the north) and a further two at RAF Coningsby (to cover London and the south). At any given time, the crews are ready to scramble within minutes of receiving the call, and, if necessary, shoot down any aircraft being used as a terrorist weapon.

Their duty-day lasts for 24 hours. As the duty crew arrives, the guys receive an intelligence briefing and change into their flying gear, with equipment never more than an arm's reach away. They'll even sleep fully kitted up in their immersion suits – it saves seconds if they have to scramble. Crews aim to launch their Typhoons as quickly as possible and they practise regularly to keep up their reaction times.

The QRA buildings are sited next to the Hardened Aircraft Shelters (HAS) containing the fuelled and ready jets. There is a crew room,

bedrooms and a common room with TV and shelves piled high with books, magazines, newspapers and DVDs – anything to help while away the hours.

In an old cold war bunker, computers and radar feeds from around the country scan Britain's crowded airways. The responsibility for 24-hour surveillance of the UK's airspace rests with RAF Boulmer in Northumbria and in the base's newly refurbished control room,

fighter controllers interpret the signals from the thousands of aircraft that are flying above UK airspace at any one time; if any lose contact or are hijacked, they will warn the fighters to stand by. The most senior of a small group of cabinet ministers can be patched into the command circuit within seconds. What unfolds over subsequent minutes will dictate whether the order to scramble is given.

The scramble is an adrenaline-charged sprint, redolent of those early summer days during the Battle of Britain when Spitfire and Hurricane pilots would lounge fully-kitted up near their aircraft, awaiting the tannoy's call to arms. Seconds count and even as today's QRA aircrew run to their aircraft, their ground crews will be on-station preparing the aircraft for rapid departure. Within minutes of the call, the Typhoons are airborne, the ground falling away as they climb and accelerate at up to twice the speed of sound to meet whatever in-bound threat has been assessed a danger to British airspace. Their first task is to get alongside a suspect aircraft, and become the eyes of the decision maker. Then, if needed, they are his finger on the trigger.

RAF fighters have been scrambled to intercept commercial jets in UK airspace more than 150 times since 9/11; fortunately the incidents have mainly involved aircraft with faulty systems or pilot error. But if any aircraft proves to be a threat, the Typhoons are equipped to shoot them down with missiles or cannons. It is a last resort – any decision to destroy an airliner would be taken at the highest level.

Every encounter with an airliner is tense. Says one QRA pilot who wishes to remain anonymous, 'We've had a couple of incidents

where somebody has lowered their table to find a note saying there's a bomb on board as a 'joke'. Recently, we had a US carrier which got airborne, heading north out of London; there was another jet from his airline due to take off shortly after. Without reference to anybody, the pilot of the first jet did a circuit to wait for his mate's aircraft to catch up. So there's a situation where an aircraft departs the UK for the US, and carries out an unauthorised orbit where it starts to turn back towards London. To the controllers, it looks like a prospective terrorist incident unfolding and the signal comes down to us. That's a good example of what we get called up to investigate. We'll fly alongside the airliner and get the pilot's attention if they've lost comms or can't be raised on the radio.

'Shooting down an airliner is a scenario you hope never happens. But when it's 330 people and two hijackers against thousands on the ground in London or, say, Canary Wharf, there's no question; everyone hopes it will never happen to them and that's how you deal with it but, at the end of the day, it's what we're here for.'

Fl Lt Nick Graham, a pilot with 29(R) Squadron based at RAF Coningsby says, 'When we're on Q, we get called to the cockpit several times a day so it's pretty busy in that regard although, more often than not, you're called to the cockpit and that's it. You're stood down before you get airborne 90% of the time because whatever the problem was – an aircraft out of contact or on the wrong flight path, or whatever – has been resolved.

A couple of the guys in 11 Squadron were scrambled in April 2012 to intercept a civilian helicopter in the Oxford area whose pilot had used a wrong frequency and sent out the emergency signal that indicates an aircraft has either been hijacked or "gone rogue". That one made the news because the two Typhoons went supersonic over land. Thousands of people heard the sonic boom, and thinking it was an explosion, inundated the MoD with calls. Authority for the guys to go supersonic would have been authorised by London Military Air Traffic Control – it's only allowed in exceptional circumstances over land and, in this case, because the helicopter was transmitting the hijack code, the circumstances were exceptional.

In this kind of scenario, where you're intercepting a light aircraft or helicopter, you obviously have to take care because the wash from our engines could literally throw them out of the sky. We'll usually approach from the left and fly alongside to get the crew's attention. When we overshoot instead of turning away to the left, we turn over the top, putting our jet efflux away from his aircraft. In the case of a helicopter, you give him extra room – you don't want to go directly over the top of the disc otherwise you'll destroy his lift and he'll drop out the sky.

Typhoons and their predecessor Tornado F3s have been scrambled to intercept suspect airliners over 100 times since 9/11, according to the MoD. Many of these incidents go unreported, and although there are no detailed accounts available relating to the occasions that Typhoons have been scrambled, there are a number of reports covering earlier incidents to which Tornados responded.

26 September 2004: RAF Tornado F3s were scrambled to intercept an Olympic Airways flight traveling from Athens to New York's JFK airport after threats of a bomb on board. The plane, with its 301 passengers, was re-routed to Stansted airport in Essex where the aircraft was kept in a secure holding area until expert search teams declared the plane safe. The dramatic chain of events was sparked after *Ethnos*, a Greek daily newspaper, received three anonymous telephone warnings, which referred to Iraq.

31 October 2003: An RAF Tornado was scrambled to intercept a British Airways jet feared to have been hijacked. The fighter took off from RAF Coningsby after French air traffic controllers lost radio contact with the Gatwick-bound Boeing 737 for 25 minutes. Contact was re-established over Barkway, Herts and the 80 passengers were unaware of the drama, blamed on a radio fault.

4 October 2002: RAF fighters were scrambled to intercept a British Airways jet in a major terrorist alert at 25,000ft after two passengers were reportedly overheard plotting to storm the cockpit. The captain of Flight BA228 from Baltimore alerted air traffic controllers and the Tornado F3 jets were launched from RAF Coningsby, roaring to within 200ft of the Heathrow-bound flight. After the plane landed safely at Heathrow, Scotland Yard officers removed the men from the aircraft at gunpoint, but they later concluded that no offence had been committed and the two, both American citizens, were allowed to leave.

Appendix A

Glossary of Terms

ACS: Armament Control System. Manages weapons selection and firing and monitors weapon status.

AMRAAM: Advanced Medium-Range Air-to-Air Missile. A modern beyond-visual-range missile capable of all-weather day-and-night operations.

APU: Auxiliary Power Unit. A device on the Typhoon that provides energy for functions other than propulsion. Its primary purpose is to provide power to start the engines and to run accessories while the engines are shut down.

ASRAAM: Advanced Short-Range Air-to-Air Missile. A high-speed, highly manoeuvrable, heat-seeking, air-to-air missile, designed as a 'fire-and-forget' weapon, able to counter intermittent target obscuration in cloud as well as sophisticated infra-red counter measures.

AWACS: An airborne radar system designed to detect aircraft, ships and vehicles at long ranges, and control and command the battle space in an air engagement by directing fighter and attack aircraft. Performed by Boeing Sentry E-3D aircraft operated by the RAF.

Air-to-air: Typhoon involved or configured as a fighter aircraft, to protect the air space.

Air-to-air refuelling: Also known as aerial fuelling or 'tanking', this is the process of transferring fuel from one aircraft (the tanker) to another (the receiver) during flight. The procedure allows the receiving aircraft to remain airborne longer, extending its range or loiter time on station.

Air-to-ground: Typhoon configured for the ground attack role.

Air brake: A type of flight control surface located just behind the Typhoon's cockpit that lifts to increase drag or increase the angle of approach during landing.

Angle of attack: The difference between where the wing is pointed and the direction of the air flowing over the wing.

Attitude: The attitude of an aircraft in flight refers to the inclination of its three axes to the relative wind, or its position relative to the earth such as straight and level, climbing and descending.

Boroscope: Also, Borescope. An optical device consisting of a rigid or flexible tube with an eyepiece on one end and an objective lens on the other linked together by a relay optical system. Used for inspection work where the area to be inspected is inaccessible by other means

Brimstone: An advanced air-to-ground radar-guided weapon derived from the US Army's Hellfire AGM-114F missile. It is deployed in RAF service on a pylon-mounted launching rack that contains three missiles. Powered by a rocket motor, it can seek and destroy targets at long range.

CAS: Chief of the Air Staff.

Chord: The measurement from the leading edge of a wing to the trailing edge. The term is also applied to the airfoils in a jet engine.

Close Air Support: Air action by fixed or rotary winged aircraft against hostile targets that are close to friendly forces. Requires detailed integration of each air mission with the fire and movement of these forces.

Dry Heat/Dry Thrust: Refers to an engine's power/thrust without the use of reheat, or afterburners.

Doppler Radar: A specialised radar that makes use of the Doppler Effect to produce speed data about moving objects. It works by beaming a microwave signal towards the target, then listening and analysing how the frequency of the returned signal has been altered by the object's motion.

ECM: Electronic Counter Measures. An electronic device designed to trick or deceive radar, sonar or other detection systems. Used both offensively and defensively to deny targeting information to an enemy.

Enhanced Paveway II: A laser-guided 450kg bomb based on the Paveway II with a modified guidance system. Fully autonomous where cloud cover obscures the target. In these instances, it is steered to the target using GPS data and guidance from its on-board inertial navigation unit.

Fast Air: Offensive military jet aircraft such as the Tornado GR4 or Typhoon FGR4.

F-16 Fighting Falcon: A multi-role jet fighter aircraft developed by General Dynamics for the United States Air Force (USAF). Introduced in 1978, the F-16 is scheduled to remain in service with USAF until 2025. The planned replacement is the F-35A version of the Lockheed Martin F-35 Lightning II

F/A-18 Hornet: A US twin-engine supersonic, all-weather carrier-capable multi-role fighter jet, designed to dogfight and attack ground targets. Built by McDonnell Douglas, it was introduced into service in 1983.

F-22 Raptor: A single-seat, twin-engine fifth-generation super-manoeuvrable fighter aircraft with stealth technology. Entered into service with the USAF in 2005.

F-35 Lightning II: A family of single-seat, single-engine, fifth-generation multi-role fighters under development to perform ground attack, reconnaissance and air defence missions with stealth capability. Due to enter service with the RAF and Royal Navy in 2020.

GBU: Guide Bomb Unit or smart bomb.

G-force: The 'G' stands for gravitational and refers to the acceleration of an object relative to free-fall. Despite its accepted

148

RAF TYPHOON MANUAL

use, the term G-force is technically incorrect as it refers to a measure of acceleration, not force.

HEAT: High Explosive Anti-Tank. An explosive shaped charge that on impact creates a very high-velocity jet of metal in a state of superplasticity that can punch through solid armour.

INS: Inertial Navigation System. A navigation aid that uses a computer, accelerometers and gyroscopes to continuously calculate via dead reckoning the position, direction and speed of a moving object without the need for external references.

Intel: Intelligence.

ISTAR: Intelligence, Surveillance, Target Acquisition and Reconnaissance, a practice that links several battlefield functions together to assist a combat force in employing its sensors and managing the information they gather.

JENGO: Junior ENGineering Officer

MQ-9 Reaper: A medium-to-high altitude, long-endurance remotely-piloted hunter-killer aircraft system. Although its primary mission is to act as an Intelligence, Surveillance and Reconnaissance (ISR) asset, it can provide armed support to forces on the ground and, if required, engage emerging targets. Normally armed with two GBU-12 500lb laser-guided bombs and four AGM-114 Hellfire missiles.

MIDS: A high-capacity digital information distribution system allowing the secure and jam-resistant exchange of real-time data between a wide variety of users, including all the components of a tactical air force, and where appropriate, land and naval forces.

Mach: Unit of speed relative to the speed of sound. Mach 1.0 is the speed of sound, around 1,225km/h (the value can vary according to atmospheric conditions).

NATO: An alliance of countries from North America and Europe committed to fulfilling the goals of the North Atlantic Treaty signed on 4 April 1949. It is constituted on a system of collective defence whereby its member states agree to mutual defence in response to an attack by any external party.

NVG: Night Vision Goggles. An optical instrument that magnifies available light by 50,000 times.

NETMA: The NATO Eurofighter and Tornado Management Agency, prime customer created by partner nations for the Eurofighter and Tornado.

OC: Officer Commanding – the Wing Commander in charge of a Squadron.

OCU: Operational Conversion Unit Squadrons within the Royal Air Force. Training units that prepare aircrew for operations on a particular type of aircraft.

Operation Herrick: British codename for all military operations in Afghanistan.

QRA: Quick Reaction Alert. Often abbreviated to 'Q', it refers to the RAF's 24/7, 365-day defence of British airspace. Typhoon FGR4s stand ready-armed with crews on permanent standby to launch and intercept any perceived airborne threats.

RAF Regiment: The RAF's own military corps responsible for Force Protection, airfield defence, forward air control and parachute capability.

RoE: Rules of Engagement. Laws set by a country's government laying down rules for the use and proportionality of arms and military force.

RPG: Soviet-designed Rocket Propelled Grenade. A shoulder-launched rocket with a powerful grenade warhead.

Reheat: Also known as 'afterburning'. Refers to an increase in thrust from the engine achieved by injecting fuel directly into the jet's exhaust gasses. It is generally used for take-off and combat situations. Jet engines are referred to as operating 'wet' when reheat is being used and 'dry' when not.

Rotation: The moment an aircraft lifts up from the runway and takes off, actioned by the pilot applying back pressure to the control stick.

Scope Creep: Uncontrolled changes or continuous growth in a project's scope.

SENGO: The Senior ENGineering Officer.

Stealth Technology: A sub-discipline of military tactics and passive electronic countermeasures which cover a range of techniques to make aircraft and missiles less visible (ideally invisible) to radar, infrared, sonar and other detection methods.

Stratosphere: The second major layer of earth's atmosphere, just above the troposphere, and below the mesosphere. It is situated from about 6 miles to 30 miles above the earth's surface at moderate latitudes.

Supercruise: The sustained supersonic flight of an aircraft performed efficiently and without the use of afterburners. The Typhoon can supercruise at Mach 1.5.

Swing-role: An aircraft that can accomplish both air-to-air and air-to-surface roles on the same mission and swing between these roles instantly.

Thermobaric: Enhanced blast Hellfire missile carried by the Army's Apache AH1 Attack Helicopter, and the MQ-9 Reaper operated by the RAF.

Tornado F3: The RAF's fighter-variant of the Tornado. Introduced in 1985, it was never tested in combat operations. Retired from service in March 2011 and replaced by the Typhoon.

Tornado GR4: An air-to-ground, variable geometry, two-seat, day-or-night, all-weather attack aircraft, operated by the Royal Air Force. Capable of delivering a wide variety of weapons.

Transducer: A device that converts one form of energy to another.

Troposphere: The lowest portion of earth's atmosphere, it contains approximately 80% of the atmosphere's mass and 99% of its water vapour. Its average depth is approximately 11 miles in the middle latitudes.

UAV: Unmanned Aerial Vehicle such as the MQ-9 Reaper. An aircraft without a human pilot on board, its flight is under the remote control of a pilot on the ground or in another vehicle.

Vane: A plane surface or any of a number of blades or plates attached radially to a rotating drum or cylinder such as in a jet engine that move or are moved by air.

Wingman: The other aircraft in a pair.

For further information about the people, history, structure, role, equipment and operations of the Royal Air Force, please visit www.raf.mod.uk

Appendix B

Design features and performance

Performance:
- Two EuroJet EJ200 turbofan engines, each delivering 60kN (13,490lb) in dry power and 90kN (20,250lb) with reheat
- Maximum speed of Mach 2.0
- Runway requirement of 700m (2,300ft)
- G limits +9 to −3
- Brakes off to 35,000ft and Mach 1.5 in under 150 seconds
- Brakes off to lift off in under 8 seconds (with full internals and missiles)
- 200 knots to Mach 1.0 (at low level) in 30 seconds
- Supercruise capability and dry power acceleration from sub to supersonic

Mass:
- Basic Mass Empty 11,000kg (24,250lb)
- Normal maximum take-off mass 23,500kg (50,700lb)

External Dimensions:
- Wing span 10.95m (35ft 11in)
- Wing aspect ratio 2.2
- Overall length 15.96m (52ft 4in)
- Overall height 5.28m (17ft 4in)
- Wing area 50.0m^2 (538sq ft)

Weapons and stores:
- Internally mounted 27mm Mauser cannon
- 13 external stores stations: five (including one optional wet) under fuselage and four (including one optional wet) under each wing
- Four AMRAAM under fuselage in semi-conformal carriage configuration
- Mix of Advanced Medium Range Air-to-Air missiles (AMRAAM) and Advanced Short-Range Air-to-Air Missiles (ASRAAM) carried externally
- Full range of Air-to-Surface weaponry including laser-guided bomb and unguided bombs

Index